Winning the War
Against
Radical Islam

Robert A. Morey

Christian Scholars Press

Winning the War Against Radical Islam

Robert A. Morey
Christian Scholars Press
1350 E. Flamingo Rd., Suite 97
Las Vegas, NV 88119

Printed in the United States of America
© 2002 by Robert A. Morey

ISBN 1-931230-08-0

Library of Congress Catalog Number: [pending].

ABOUT THE AUTHOR

In contrast to the dozens of "overnight" experts on Islam that have suddenly appeared since Sep. 11, 2001, Dr. Robert Morey has been writing and lecturing on Islam for over twenty years and has a doctorate in Islamic Studies.

He is an internationally recognized scholar in the fields of comparative religions, the cults, and the occult as well as on Islam. He is the author of over forty books, some of which have been translated into Spanish, Swedish, Hungarian, Norwegian, Dutch, German, French, Italian, Chinese, Turkish and Farsi. He is scholar in residence with the Research and Education Foundation and the Executive Director of Faith Defenders, the #1 ministry in the world today confronting Islam and defending the Christian Faith.

For a full listing of his books and tapes, call Faith Defenders at 1-800-41-TRUTH or visit his website at www.faithdefenders.com.

TABLE OF CONTENTS

Introduction

INTRODUCTION

As World War II turned against Japan, a "Divine Wind" of suicide warriors swarmed out of Japan against the forces of the United States. The unthinkable became a nightmare as Japanese pilots crashed their planes into American ships. Suicidal Japanese soldiers and even civilians blew themselves up to destroy American targets on the ground. Rather than surrender, Japanese soldiers and officers disemboweled themselves by cutting open their own abdomen. What could possibly motivate such fanaticism? Why were so many Japanese willing to commit suicide?

The answer was found in the Japanese religion of Emperor worship. The religious belief that the Emperor of Japan was God not only motivated the Kamikaze pilots and the ritual of Seppuku (also known as hari-kari), but it was also the very heart and soul of the entire Japanese War effort.

Emperor worship was indoctrinated into the Japanese people beginning in kindergarten. Children sang and danced about how wonderful it would be to die for the divine Emperor. Americans were viewed as Christians and were the focus of special hatred and ridicule. Emperor worship was superior to the religion of the crucified Carpenter.

In order to further its war against America, the Japanese government sent thousands of secret agents into the United States disguised as simple immigrants. Our "open door" policy allowed both Japan and Germany to infiltrate America with ease.

a

The majority of Shinto temples built in the United States were actually terrorist cells set up by the government of Japan. Religious freedom was used to hide their anti-American activities. The temples were secretly built with funds from the Japanese government funneled through American Japanese citizens and companies.

Since the average American did not know the Japanese language and since the Japanese people in America seemed to be peaceful, no one realized the danger they posed to America.

The United States president and military advisors had a dilemma before them. Since the root of Japanese militancy was the Shinto religion, they had to face the fact that unless they addressed the religion that motivated the suicide pilots, the War would drag on and on.

Did the President of the United States publicly proclaim that the religion of Shintoism was a peaceful and wonderful religion? Did he attend a Shinto temple and bow in worship before a picture of the Emperor? Did he state that all religions worship the same universal God? Did government officials rush to announce that the religion of Emperor Worship had been hijacked by terrorists and perverted into a violent religion? Did they threaten to prosecute any American citizen who made anti-Shinto comments?

The President and his military advisors clearly understood that the religion of Shintoism was the root problem. Thus the decision was made to attack the religion because it was the ultimate cause of all the death and destruction connected with the war with Japan. Government agents burst into Shinto temples and seized all the records they found. They rounded up Japanese agents and put them into jail.

So many American Japanese were involved in anti-American activities or expressed pro-Japan sentiments that the bold decision was made to intern all the Japanese in America. While it is easy to criticize this action today, the U.S. government did what it had to do to protect the lives and property of Americans. If the Japanese had not been rounded up and interned in camps, one shudders to think of all the acts of terrorism that would have happened.

When the time came for Japan to surrender, part of the terms of surrender set up by the United States required the Emperor to go on national radio and declare that he was NOT God. In other words, the Emperor was forced to renounce the religion of Shintoism that had worshipped him as God.

As the Japanese people heard their Emperor admit that the religion of Shintoism was a lie, some fainted, others wept, and some committed suicide. They had believed in the divinity of the Emperor and in his name had committed horrific acts of violence and carnage against innocent civilians throughout Asia. In the name of their god they had waged war against America and had tortured American prisoners of war in ways that were so terrible and sadistic that people today would not believe them possible.

The same could be said of the religion of Nazism that motivated the German people to conquer the world for Hitler. Did our government officials proclaim that Nazism was a peaceful religion? Did they claim that the Nazis were a peaceful people and that America welcomed all Nazis who wanted to immigrate to this country? Were they so stupid as to pretend that Nazism had been hijacked by a few individuals and that the U.S. was only going after Hitler and his chief officers? Did the media censor anyone who was brave enough to say that Nazism was an evil and wicked religion?

America won WWII because it was gloriously insensitive to the feelings of the Japanese, the Germans and the Italians. The liberal "politically correct" crowd was not allowed to hobble the American war effort. But what about today?

Sad to say, the religion of liberalism has made tremendous inroads into the government of the United States. For all practical purposes, it is now the state religion of America and dogmatically taught in the public school system. This religion teaches such doctrines as universalism, the idea that all religions worship the same universal God under different names. It also teaches relativism, the idea that there are no absolute standards of good or evil, true or false.

Liberalism claims that religion *per se* is a matter of personal preference or taste like one's choice of vanilla or chocolate ice cream. Such choices cannot be placed in the categories of truth or morals. Thus all religions are "true" and "good" in the sense of being a non-truth and non-moral issue of personal taste. It is thus politically incorrect to say that Islam or any other religion is "false" or "evil" because religion is not a matter of truth or morals.

The absurdity of liberalism is that it exempts itself from its own dogma of relativism. It demands that you view their doctrines and beliefs (such as universalism and relativism) as being absolutely true! It is thus self-refuting and hypocritical in its very core.

d

Radical Islam does not buy into the religion of liberalism. It believes that it is the only one true religion on the planet and that it has a moral duty from its god, Allah, to force the entire world to adopt Islamic law. The call of the minaret is that no one has the *right* to worship any other god than Allah or to follow the teachings of any prophet other than Muhammad. It is exclusive and intolerant of any other religion. To Bin Ladin or any other fundamentalist Muslim, all other religions are false and evil in an absolute sense. Thus, they must be destroyed.

Liberalism is absolutely impotent to fight Islam because it cannot condemn it as false or evil. If all religions are true, than the religion of Bin Ladin is true. If his religion tells him to destroy the lives and property of non-Muslims, his religion cannot be condemned as false or evil.

The smart liberals recognize their inability to deal with Islam. So they pretend that fundamentalist Muslims are not following the "real" teachings of Islam. They are guilty of assuming a false premise as their starting point.

All religions are peaceful.

Islam is a religion.

Therefore Islam is a peaceful religion.

Liberals repeat this mantra on TV, radio or in the pulpit in the Hessian hope that if they can chant it long enough and loud enough, most people will be stupid enough to buy into it. And, sad to say, most people have been stupid enough to fall for it!

The liberal fails to realize that his starting point is not factually true. The New Age religion of Jim Jones was both false and evil as evidenced by the pile of corpses in his jungle camp. The Hindu cult of Kali is both false and evil

e

because it calls for the murder of people as an act of devotion to the goddess. Occultic and satanic religions that kidnap children and use them as human sacrifices do not fit the liberal mantra. A "reality check" reveals that not all religions are peaceful. Some can be downright dangerous.

If you are a brainwashed liberal reading this book, I understand that you are infuriated at this point because, like the child in the story about the emperor who had no clothes, I have exposed your meaningless mantra, "All religions are peaceful." The first step in winning the battle against radical Islam is to abandon your naïve attachment to Liberalism. Why? It renders you incapable of condemning the religion of Bin Ladin as a false, evil or violent religion. As long as you are committed to relativism, you cannot judge what radical Islam does in the name of its god.

I therefore issue a call for liberals to stop being so narrow-minded, closed-minded, bigoted and intolerant! Open yourself up to new ideas and new experiences. Break free of the politically correct status quo. Be a rebel and turn your world upside down by accepting the fact that all religions are not true, good or peaceful.

PART ONE

JUST THE FACTS PLEASE

"We're not attacking Islam but Islam is attacking us. The God of Islam is not the same God. He's not the Son of God of the Christian or the Judeo-Christian Faith. It's a different God and I believe it is a very evil and wicked religion."

Franklin Graham

CHAPTER ONE

WHO IS THIS ALLAH?

INTRODUCTION

The art of asking questions is the very soul and substance of all scholarship and research. Asking questions is the only way to find out the Truth about any religion including Islam. We must always remember that the Truth is never afraid of the spotlight of investigation.

In order to find an answer to the topic of our dialogue, we must be willing to ask some very hard questions. We must probe deeply into the sources of Islam. We must be willing to let history and science answer our questions instead of blindly following the dictates of dogmatism.

THE QUR'AN AND QUESTIONS

We recognize that this will be especially hard for Muslims because they are forbidden by the Qur'an to ask questions about their own faith! They are warned that if they start asking questions, they may lose their faith in Islam!

> "O ye who believe! Ask not questions about things which if made plain to you, may cause you trouble. Some people before you did ask questions, and on that account lost their faith" (Surah 5:101-102).

In his famous commentary on the Qur'an, Maududi warns Muslims not to probe too deeply into Islam.

"The Holy Prophet himself forbade people to ask questions …so do not try to probe into such things."

The Meaning of the Qur'an, Maududi, vol. III, pgs. 76-77

The questions were not the problem. When the answers were "made plain" it caused people to lose their faith in Islam. Whenever people tell you not to ask questions because if you find the answers you will lose your faith in them, they are trying to hide something.

Bukhari's Hadith tells us how Muhammad responded to those who asked him questions:

"The Prophet was asked about things which he did not like, and when the questioner insisted, the Prophet got angry" (vol. 1, no. 92).

"The Prophet got angry and his cheeks or his face became red" (vol.1, no. 91).

"Allah has hated you…[for] asking too many questions" (vol. 2, no. 555; and vol. 3, no. 591).

We must ask ourselves, "What kind of god is Allah who hates people for asking questions? This is not like the God of the Bible who encourages us to ask, to seek and to knock! Why is Muhammad pictured as hating those who asked him questions? Why were people warned not to ask questions? What is Islam trying to hide? Is Islam so weak that merely asking questions threatens to destroy it? Do Muslims assume that blind faith is the way to Islam?

THE FREEDOM TO QUESTION

Thankfully, we live in a wonderful country where we are free to ask all the questions we want. We are free to probe deeply into the sources of Islam, its god and its religious ceremonies, until we find the answer. Indeed, any Muslim who fails to ask questions about the sources of the Qur'an and Islam will be guilty of blind fanaticism and gross ignorance. He should remember that if his religion is true, then there is nothing to fear from asking questions.

THE INFIDEL'S CHALLENGE

According to the Qur'an, the infidels of Muhammad's day rejected the Qur'an because it was composed of old stories and myths.

> "But the unbelievers say, 'This is nothing but a lie which he has forged, and others have helped him do it ...tales of the ancients, which he has caused to be written; and they are dictated before him morning and evening'" (Surah 25:4-5).

The accusation is quite clear: The Qur'an is not a "revelation" brought down out of heaven to Muhammad but it is a forgery composed of previously existing stories. The source of the material found in the Qur'an was the main point of their accusation.

ALLAH'S RESPONSE

How did the authors of the Qur'an handle this accusation? Surprisingly, all they did was attack the character of those who made the accusation and then simply repeat that the Qur'an was brought down from heaven.

"In truth, it is they who have put forward an iniquity and falsehood" (Surah 25:4).

"Say: 'The Qur'an was sent down by Him who knows the mystery that is in the heavens'" (Surah 25:6).

In his commentary, Yusuf Ali states,

"In their misquided arrogance they say, 'We have heard such things before: they are pretty tales which have come down from ancient times: they are good for amusement, but who takes them seriously?'" (3057).

"The answer is that the Qur'an teaches spiritual knowledge of what is ordinarily hidden from men's sight, and such knowledge can only come from God to Whom alone is known the Mystery of the whole Creation."

The question of the sources of the Qur'an is crucial to whether Islam is true or false. Why? The famous Muslim commentator Maududi explains,

"Apparently, this is a weighty argument. For there can be no greater proof of the 'fraud' of Prophethood than to specify its source. But it looks strange that no argument has been put forward to refute this charge except a mere denial, as if to say, 'Your charge is an impudent lie: you are cruel and unjust to bring such a false charge against Our Messenger, for the Qur'an is the Word of Allah Who knows all the secrets in the heavens and the earth.'"

The Meaning of the Qur'an, Maududi,
Vol.III, pgs.178-179.

The question of whether Islam derived its beliefs and
ceremonies from heaven or from earth is crucial. If it
obtained its god, its rites and its doctrines from pre-existing
pagan religions, then the claim that it was "brought down
from heaven" falls to the ground.

FOUNDATIONAL PRINCIPLES

1. We can all agree on this common ground: The
   Qur'an is *literature*.

2. Our interpretation of the Qur'an is subject to the
   same rules of analysis and exegesis that govern the
   interpretation of any other piece of literature:
   grammar, syntax, literary context, historical
   context and cultural context.

3. One literary rule is that when a book refers to
   things without explaining them to the readers, the
   author is assuming that these things are so well
   known that no explanation is needed.

4. The Qur'an refers to gods, people, places and
   things which are nowhere explained or defined
   within the Qur'an itself.

5. The authors of the Qur'an assumed that everyone
   already knew of these things and thus no
   explanation was needed.

6. There are many passages in the Qur'an which
   would be unintelligible if we did not go outside of
   the Qur'an to the historical and cultural context of
   pre-Islamic Arabia. Such surahs as "The Blind
   Man" (80), "The Elephant" (105), etc., are

unintelligible if recourse is not made to historical sources.

7. All scholars use pre-Islamic history to explain the contents of the Qur'an.

8. What kind of literature is the Qur'an? Is it rational discourse or historical narrative? Is it a book of songs or poems? What is it? The authors of the Qur'an tell us that it is primarily composed of "pretty stories". Indeed, if we removed all the "pretty stories" from the text of the Qur'an, it would be reduced to a few pages of threats and warnings.

> "We relate to you the most pretty stories
> in what we reveal to you in this Qur'an"
> (Surah 12:3).

9. From where did these "stories" originate? Were they "brought down" from heaven or were they derived from old myths and legends?

Many scholars are agreed that the stories found in the Qur'an were derived from the legends and myths of the Arabs, Jews, Persians and Christians. In other words, they did not come from heaven, but from earth. Their source is not Allah, but human storytellers. This is why many scholars view the Qur'an as a fanciful book of ancient tales.

This will not come as a surprise to anyone who actually reads the Qur'an. It is primarily composed of old fables and myths that convolute the names, dates, events and places of biblical and secular history into incoherent fantasies. Such fantastic stories as the youths in the cave, the she-camel, the monkey people and the night journey are only faint garbled reflections of the original tales.

Example: Yusuf Ali's translation and commentary on the Qur'an is well known and accepted all over the world. In his comments on the text, he traces the stories of the Qur'an back to the original Arab, Jewish, Persian or Christian legends from which they were derived. He does not deny the earthly sources of the Qur'an. Instead, he documents them!

If the Qur'an is a confused and jumbled record of ancient "stories" drawn from the various nations conquered by the Arabs, this becomes the most serious threat to Islam's claim of divine revelation. Maududi was right. Once we identify the sources of the Qur'an, it is no longer a revelation.

YUSUF ALI'S TRANSLATION AND COMMENTARY

Surah	Verse	Source of Story
2	60	Jewish and Arab legends
	65	Jewish legends
	125	Arab legends
	189	Arab legends
	194	Arab legends
	196	Arab legends
	197	Arab legends
	198	Arab legends
	199	Arab legends
	200	Arab legends

	259	Jewish legend
3	49	Christian legend
7	65	Arab legends
	73	Arab legends
	85	Arab legends
11	59	Arab legends
18	9	Christian legend
	110	Persian source
74	32	Arab legends

10. It is thus proper and appropriate to apply the question of sources to the god of Islam. Did Islam derive its god from revelation or from previously existing sources?

GENERAL QUESTIONS

The following general and specific questions can be answered by reading the documentation that follows them. The standard reference works on Islam and its rituals are virtually unanimous in supplying the same answers.

- Is it possible to believe that you are worshipping the true God when you are actually worshipping a false god?

- Do most religions have sacred books that claim that the God, gods or goddesses revealed in their books are true?

- Does merely claiming that you worship the true God prove that you are in fact worshipping the true God?

- Does the Qur'an claim that Allah is the true God?

- Is it possible that the Qur'an could be in error and thus Allah is a false god?

- Is it possible that Islam derived the name "Allah" from pre-Islamic sources?

SPECIFIC QUESTIONS

- Does the Qur'an define the word "Allah" before using it for the first time?

- Was the name "Allah" revealed for the first time in the Qur'an?

- Does the Qur'an assume that its readers have already heard of "Allah"?

- Should we look into pre-Islamic Arabian history to see who "Allah" was before Muhammad?

- According to Muslim tradition, was Muhammad born into a Christian family and tribe?

- Was he born into a Jewish family or tribe?

- What religion was his family and tribe?

- What was the name of his pagan father?

- Did Muhammad participate in the pagan ceremonies of Mecca?

- Did the Arabs in pre-Islamic times worship 360 gods?

- Did the pagan Arabs worship the sun, moon and the stars?

"It will be noticed that the sun and the moon and the five planets got identified with a living deity, god or goddesses, with the qualities of its own.

"Moon worship was equally popular in various forms...

"It may be noted that the moon was a male Divinity in ancient India; it was also a male Divinity in ancient Semitic religion, and the Arabic word for the moon (qamar) is of the masculine gender. On the other hand, the Arabic word for the sun (shama) is of the feminine gender. The pagan Arabs evidently looked upon the sun as a goddess and the moon as a god.

"If Wadd and Suwa represented Man and Woman, they might well represent the astral worship of the moon and the sun...

"The Pagan deities best known in the Ka'ba and round about Mecca were Lat, Uzza and Manat.... They were all female goddesses."

The Forms of Pagan Worship,
Yusuf Ali, pgs. 1619-1623

In his explanation of why the Qur'an swears by the moon in Surah74:32, "Nay verily by the Moon," Yusuf Ali comments,

"The moon was worshipped as a deity in times of darkness" (fn. 5798, pg. 1644).

1. Did the Arabs build temples to the Moon-god?

2. Did different Arab tribes give the Moon-god different names/titles?

3. What were some of the names/titles? Sin, Hubul, Ilumquh, Al-ilah.

4. Was the title "al-ilah" (the god) used of the Moon-god?

5. Was the word "Allah" derived from "al-ilah"?

6. Was the pagan "Allah" a high god in a pantheon of deities?

7. Was he worshipped at the Kabah?

8. Was Allah only one of many Meccan pagan gods?

9. Did they place a statue of Hubul on top of the Kabah?

10. At that time was Hubul considered the Moon-god?

11. Was the Kabah called the "house of the Moon-god"?

12. Did the name "Allah" eventually replace that of Hubul as the name of the Moon-god?

13. Did the pagans call the Kabah the "house of Allah"?

14. Did the pagans develop religious rites in connection with the worship of their gods?

15. Did the pagans practice the Pilgrimage, the Fast of Ramadan, running around the Kabah seven times,

kissing the black stone, shaving the head, animal sacrifices, running up and down two hills, throwing stones at the devil, snorting water in and out the nose, praying several times a day toward Mecca, giving alms, Friday prayers, etc.?

16. Did Muhammad command his followers to participate in these pagan ceremonies while the pagans were still in control of Mecca? Yusuf Ali, in footnote #214, pg. 78, states that Muhammad and his followers joined the pagans in their rituals at the Kabah.

17. Did Islam go on to adopt these pagan religious rites?

> "The whole of the [pagan] pilgrimage was spiritualized in Islam..."
>
> Yusuf Ali, fn. 223, pg. 80

18. Were al-Lat, al-Uzza and Manat called the "daughers of Allah"? Yusuf Ali explains in footnoe 5096, pg. 1445, that Lat, Uzza and Manat were known as "the daughters of God [Allah]".

19. Did the Qur'an in Surah 53:19-20 at one point tell Muslims to worship al-Lat, al-Uzza and Manat?

20. Have those verses been "abrogated" out of the present Qur'an?

21. Why are they called the "Satanic Verses"?

22. Was the crescent moon an ancient pagan symbol of the Moon-god throughout the ancient world?

23. Was it the religious symbol of the Moon-god in Arabia?

24. Were stars also used as pagan symbols of the daughters of Allah?

25. Did the Jews or the Christians in the seventh century use the crescent moon with several stars next to it as symbols of their faith?

26. Did Islam adopt the pagan crescent moon and stars as its religious symbols?

27. As Islam developed over the centuries, did it adopt pagan names, pagan ceremonies, pagan temples and pagan symbols?

28. Is it possible that most Muslims do not know the pagan sources of the symbols and rites of their own religion?

29. Are they shocked to find out the true sources of their ceremonies and stories?

30. Can Islam be the religion of Abraham if it is derived from paganism?

31. Is Islam an ancient fertility cult in monotheistic form?

32. Is the "Allah" of the Qur'an, the Christian God of Father, Son and Holy Spirit?

33. Do the Jews say that the Muslim "Allah" is YHWH?

34. Then whose god is Allah?

DOCUMENTATION

The following citations reveal that there is a general consensus among Islamic scholars that Allah was a pagan deity before Islam developed. He was only one god among a pantheon of 360 gods worshipped by the Arabs. Even if he was at times viewed as a "high god", this does not mean he was the one true God.

The word Allah was most likely derived from *al-ilah*, which had become the generic title for whatever god was considered the highest god. Each Arab tribe used *Allah* to refer to its own particular high god. This is why Hubal, the Moon-god, was the central focus of prayer at the Kabah and people prayed to Hubal using the name Allah. Different tribes preferred other names such as Sin or Ilmaqah. Allah was NEVER called YHWH or Jesus.

> "Some of the early Arabs also revered certain gods and goddessses. Although these divinities varied according to the tribe or area of the peninsula, there seems to have been a common belief in at least one of these gods: Allah, the creator of the universe. Allah was probably considered the supreme god, but, unlike the other deities beneath him, he was thought to have little involvement in the daily lives of people.
>
> Matthew S. Gordon, *Islam*,
> (Facts On File: NY: 1991, p. 16).

"Historians like Vaqqidi have said Allah was actually the chief of the 360 gods being worshipped in Arabia at the time Mohammed rose to prominence. Ibn Al-Kalbi gave 27 names of pre-Islamic deities.... Interestingly, not many Muslims want to accept that Allah was already being worshipped at the Ka'ba in Mecca by Arab pagans before Mohammed came. Some Muslims become angry when they are confronted with this fact. But

history is not on their side. Pre-Islamic literature
has proved this."

> G.J.O. Moshay, *Who Is This Allah?* (Dorchester
> House, Bucks, UK, 1994) pg. 138.

"Islam also owes the term 'Allah' to the
heathen Arabs. We have evidence that it entered
into numerous personal names in Northern Arabia
and among the Nabatians. It occurred among the
Arabs of later times, in theophorous names and on
its own."

> Ibn Warraq, *Why I Am Not A Muslim*, (Prometheus,
> Amherst, 1995) p. 42.

"In any case it is an extremely important fact
that Muhammad did not find it necessary to
introduce an altogether novel deity, but contented
himself with ridding the heathen Allah of his
companions subjecting him to a kind of dogmatic
purification."

> *Encyclopedia of Religion and Ethics*, I:664.

"The name Allah, as the Qur'an itself is
witness, was well known in pre-Islamic Arabia.
Indeed, both it and its feminine form, Allat, are
found not infrequently among the theophorous
names in inscriptions from North Africa."

> Arthur Jeffrey, ed., *Islam: Muhammad and His
> Religion*, (New York: The Liberal Arts Press,
> 1958), p. 85.

"Allah is a proper name, applicable only to
their [the Arabs'] peculiar God."

> *Encyclopedia of Religion and Ethics*, I:326.

" Allah is a pre-Islamic name...."

> *Encyclopedia of Religion and Ethics*, I:117.

"Allah is found...in Arabic inscriptions prior to Islam."

> *Encyclopedia Britannica*, I:643.

"The Arabs, before the time of Muhammad, accepted and worshipped, after a fashion, a supreme god called Allah."

> *Encyclopedia of Islam*, eds. Houtsma, Arnold, Basset, Hartman (Leiden: E.J. Brill, 1913), I:302.

"Allah was known to the pre-Islamic Arabs; he was one of the Meccan deities."

> *Encyclopedia of Islam*, ed. Gibb, I:406.

"Ilah...appears in pre-Islamic poetry.... By frequency of usage, al-ilah was contracted to allah, frequently attested to in pre-Islamic poetry."

> *Encyclopedia of Islam*, eds. Lewis, Menage, Pellat, Schacht (Leiden: E.J. Brill, 1971), II:1093.

"The name Allah goes back before Muhammed."

> *The Facts on File: Encyclopedia of World Mythology and Legend*, ed. Anthony Mercatante (New York, *The Facts on File*, 1983), I:41.

"The source of this (Allah) goes back to pre-Muslim times. Allah is not a common name meaning "God" (or a "god"), and the Muslim must use another word or form if he wishes to indicate any other than his own peculiar deity.

Encyclopedia of Religion and Ethics, (ed. Hastings), I:326.

"Allah was already known by name to the Arabs."

Henry Preserved Smith, *The Bible and Islam: or, The Influence of the Old and New Testament on the Religion of Mohammed,* (New York: Charles Scribner's Sons, 1897), p. 102.

"Allah: Perceived in pre-Islamic times as the creator of the earth and water, though not, at that time, considered monotheistically....

"Allat: Astral and tutelary goddess. Pre-Islamic.... One of three daughters of Allah."

Encyclopedia of Gods, p. 11

"Manat: Goddess. Pre-Islamic... One of the so-called daughters of Allah."

Encyclopedia of Gods, p. 156

"Allah: Originally applied to the moon; he seems to be preceded by Ilmaqah, the moon god.... Allat: the female counterpart to Allah."

Dictionary of Non-Classical Mythology, p. 7.

"Allah: Before the birth of Muhammad, Allah was known as a supreme, but not sole, God."

Oxford Dictionary of World Religions, p. 48

"Before Islam, the religions of the Arabic
world involved the worship of many spirits, called
jinn. Allah was but one of many gods worshipped
in Mecca. But then Muhammad taught the worship
of Allah as the only God, whom he identified as
the same God worshipped by Christians and
Jews."

A Short History of Philosophy, (Oxford
University Press) p. 130.

"The name Allah is also evident in
archeological and literary remains of pre-Islamic
Arabia."

Kenneth Cragg, *The Call of the Minaret*, (New
York: Oxford University Press, 1956), p. 31.

"In recent years I have become increasingly
convinced that for an adequate understanding of
the career of Muhammad and the sources of Islam
great importance must be attached to the existence
in Mecca of belief in Allah as a 'high god'. In a
sense this is a form of paganism, but it is so
different from paganism as commonly understood
that it deserves separate treatment."

William Montgomery Watt, *Muhammad's
Mecca*, p. vii.

"The use of the phrase 'the Lord of this
House' makes it likely that those Meccans who
believed in Allah as a high god – and they may
have been numerous – regarded the Ka'ba as his
shrine, even though there were images of other
gods in it. There are stories in the Sira of pagan

Meccans praying to Allah while standing beside the image of Hubal."

William Montgomery Watt, *Muhammad's Mecca*, p. 39.

"The customs of heathenism have left an indelible mark on Islam, notably in the rites of the pilgrimage (on which more will be said later), so that for this reason alone something ought to be said about the chief characteristics of Arabian paganism.

"The relation of this name, which in Babylonia and Assyria became a generic term simply meaning 'god', to the Arabian Ilah familiar to us in the form Allah, which is compounded of al, the definite article, and Ilah by eliding the vowel 'i', is not clear. Some scholars trace the name to the South Arabian Ilah, a title of the Moon god, but this is a matter of antiquarian interest...it is clear from Nabataen and other inscriptions that Allah meant 'the god'.

"The other gods mentioned in the Quran are all female deities: Al-Lat, al-Uzza, and Manat, which represented the Sun, the planet Venus, and Fortune, respectively; at Mecca they were regarded as the daughters of Allah...As Allah meant 'the god', so Al-Lat means 'the goddess'."

Alfred Guilaume, *Islam* (Penguin, 1956) pgs.6-7.

"As well as worshipping idols and spirits, found in animals, plants, rocks and water, the ancient Arabs believed in several major gods and goddesses whom they considered to hold supreme power over all things. The most famous of these were Al-Lat, Al-Uzza, Manat and Hubal. The first three were thought to be the daughters of Allah (God) and their intercessions on behalf of their worshippers were therefore of great significance.

"Hubal was associated with the Semitic god Ba'l and with Adonis or Tammuz, the gods of spring, fertility, agriculture and plenty…. Hubal's idol used to stand by the holy well inside the Sacred House. It was made of red sapphire but had a broken arm until the tribe of Quraysh, who considered him one of their major gods, made him a replacement in solid gold.

"In addition to the sun, moon and the star Al-Zuhara, the Arabs worshipped the planets— Saturn, Mercury, and Jupiter, the stars Sirius and Canopus and the constellations of Orion, Ursa Major and Minor, and the seven Pleiades.

"Some stars and planets were given human characters. According to legend, Al-Dabaran, one of the stars in the Hyades group, fell deeply in love with Al-Thurayya, the fairest of the Pleiades stars. With the approval of the Moon, he asked for her hand in marriage."

Khairt al-Saeh, *Fabled Cities, Princes & Jin From Arab Myths and Legends,* (New York: Schocken, 1985), p. 28-30.

"Along with Allah, however, they worshipped a host of lesser gods and 'daughters of Allah.'"

Encyclopedia of World Mythology and Legend,
I:61.

"It must not be assumed that since Moslems worship one God they are very close to Christians in their faith. The important thing is not the belief that God is One, but the conception that the believers have of God's character. Satan also believes and trembles! As Raymond Lull, the first great missionary to Moslems, pointed out long ago, the greatest deficiency in the Moslem religion is in its conception of God...for as we know, Jehovah the God of the Bible, known both to Jews and Christians, is revealed much differently than Allah, the god of Islam."

Howard F. Vos, Ed., Religions in a Changing
World, (Chicago, 1961), pp. 70, 71.

"Allah was the name of a god whom the Arabs worshipped many centuries before Muhammed was born."

The World Book Encyclopedia, (Chicago, 1955),
Vol. 1, p. 230.

"But history establishes beyond the shadow of doubt that even the pagan Arabs, before Mohammed's time, knew their chief god by the name of Allah and even, in a sense, proclaimed his unity.... Among the pagan Arabs this term denoted the chief god of their pantheon, the Kaaba, with its three hundred and sixty idols."

Samuel M. Zwemer, *The Moslem Doctrine of God,* (New York, 1905), pp. 24-25.

"There is no corroborative evidence whatsoever for the Qur'an's claim that the Ka'aba was initially a house of monotheist worship. Instead there certainly is evidence as far back as history can trace the sources and worship of the Ka'aba that it was thoroughly pagan and idolatrous in content and emphasis."

John Gilchrist, *The Temple, The Ka'aba, and The Christ*, (Benoni, South Africa, 1980), p. 16.

"In pre-Islamic days, called the Days of Ignorance, the religious background of the Arabs was pagan, and basically animistic. Through wells, stones, caves, springs, and other natural objects man could make contact with the deity.... At Mekka, Allah was the chief of the gods and the special deity of the Quraish, the prophet's tribe. Allah had three daughters: Al-Uzzah (Venus) most revered of all and pleased with human sacrifice; Manah, the goddess of destiny, and Al Lat, the goddess of vegetable life. Hubal and more than 300 others made up the pantheon. The central shrine at Mekka was the Kaaba, a cube-like stone structure which still stands though many times rebuilt. Imbedded in one corner is the black stone, probably a meteorite, the kissing of which is now an essential part of the pilgrimage."

John Van Ess, *Meet the Arab*, (New York, 1943), p. 29.

"...a people of Arabia, of the race of the Joktanites...the Alilai living near the Red Sea in a

district where gold is found; their name, children
of the moon, so called from the worship of the
moon, or Alilat."

*Gesenius Hebrew and Chaldee Lexicon to the
Old Testament Scriptures*, translated by Samuel
Prideaux Tregelles (Grand Rapids, MI, 1979), p.
367.

"That Islam was conceived in idolatry is
shown by the fact that many rituals performed in
the name of Allah were connected with the pagan
worship that existed before Islam. And today,
millions of Moslems pray towards Mecca where
the famous revered black stone is located.

"Before Islam, Allah was reported to be
known as:

- the supreme of a pantheon of gods.

- the name of a god whom the Arabs worshipped.

- the chief god of the pantheon.

- Ali-ilah, the god, the supreme.

- the all-powerful, all-knowing, and totally
unknowable.

- the predeterminer of everyone's life (destiny).

- the chief of the gods.

- the special deity of the Quraish.

- having three daughters: Al Uzzah (Venus),
Manah (Destiny), and Alat.

- having the idol temple at Mecca under his
name (House of Allah).

- the mate of Alat, the goddess of fate.

"Because the Ka'aba, the sacred shrine which contains the Black Stone, in Mecca was used for pagan idol worship before Islam and even called the House of Allah at that time.

"Because the rituals involved with the Islamic Pilgrimage are either identical or very close to the pre-Islamic pagan idol worship at Mecca.

"Because of other Arabian history which points to heathen worship of the sun, moon, and the stars, as well as other gods, of which I believe Allah was in some way connected to.

"This then would prove to us that Allah is not the same as the true God of the Bible whom we worship, because God never changes."

M. J. Afshari, Is Allah the Same God as the God of the Bible? pgs. 6, 8, 9.

"If a Muslim says, 'Your God and our God is the same,' either he does not understand who Allah and Christ really are, or he intentionally glosses over the deep-rooted differences."

Adb-Al Masih, Who is Allah in Islam? (Villach, Austria, Light of Life, 1985), p. 36.

"Sin. – The moon-god occupied the chief place in the astral triad. Its other two members, Shamash the sun and Istar the planet Venus, were his children. Thus it was, in effect, from the night that light had emerged…. In his physical aspect

Sin—who was venerated at Ur under the name of
Nannar—was an old man with a long beard the
color of lapis-lazuli. He normally wore a turban.
Every evening he got into his barque—which to
mortals appeared in the form of a brilliant crescent
moon—and navigated the vast spaces of the
nocturnal sky. Some people, however, believed
that the luminous crescent was Sin's weapon. But
one day the crescent gave way to a disk, which
stood out in the sky like a gleaming crown. There
could be no doubt that this was the god's own
crown; and then Sin was called 'Lord of the
Diadem'.

"These successive and regular transformations lent Sin a certain mystery. For this reason he
was considered to be 'He whose deep heart no god
can penetrate'.... Sin was also full of wisdom. At
the end of every month the gods came to consult
him and he made decisions for them.... His wife
was Ningal, 'the great Lady'. He was the father
not only of Shamash and Istar but also of a son
Nusku, the god of fire."

Larousse Encyclopedia of Mythology, (New
York, 1960), pp. 54-56.

"Allah, the Supreme Being of the
Mussulmans: Before Islam. That the Arabs,
before the time of Muhammed, accepted and
worshipped, after a fashion, a supreme god called
Allah, "the Ilah", or the god, if the form is of
genuine Arabic source; if of Aramaic, from Alaha,
"the god"—seems absolutely certain. Whether he
was an abstraction or a development from some

individual god, such as Hubal, need not here be
considered.... But they also recognized and tended
to worship more fervently and directly other
strictly subordinate gods.... It is certain that they
regarded particular deities (mentioned in 1iii. 19-
20 are al-'Ussa, Manat, or Manah, al-Lat; some
have interpreted vii, 179 as a reference to a
perversion of Allah to Allat as daughters of Allah,
vi. 100; xvi. 59; xxxvii. 149; liii. 21); they also
asserted that he had sons (vi. 100).... 'There was
no god save Allah.' This meant, for Muhammed
and the Meccans, that of all the gods whom they
worshipped, Allah was the only real deity. It took
no account of the nature of God in the abstract,
only of the personal position of Allah...ilah, the
common noun from which Allah is probably
derived...."

First Encyclopedia of Islam, E.J. Brill (New
York, 1987), p. 302

"Islam for its part ensured the survival of
these pre-Islamic constituents, endowed them with
a universal significance, and provided them with a
context within which they have enjoyed a most
remarkable longevity. Some of these significant
constituents, nomadic and sedentary, the pre-
Islamic roots which have formed the persistent
heritage, deserve to be noted and discussed.... The
pre-Islamic Pilgrimage in its essential features
survives, indeed is built into the very structure of
Islam as one of its Five Pillars of Faith."

The Cambridge History of Islam, Vol. I, ed. P.M.
Holt (Cambridge, 1970), p.27.

"The Quran (22.51/I) implies that on at least one occasion 'Satan had interposed' something in the revelation Muhammad received, and this probably refers to the incident to be described. The story is that, while Muhammad was hoping for some accommodation with the great merchants, he received a revelation mentioning the goddesses al-Lat, al-Uzza, and Manat (53.19-20, as now found), but continuing with other two (or three) verses sanctioning intercession to these deities. At some later date Muhammad received a further revelation abrogating the latter verses, but retaining the names of the goddesses, and saying it was unfair that God should have only daughters while human beings had sons."

The Cambridge History of Islam, Vol. I, ed. P.M.
Holt (Cambridge, 1970), p. 37.

"This notation at times might be very simple, as can be illustrated by such equations as the sun or winged sun for the sun-god (Sumerian, Utu; Akkadian, Shamash), a crescent moon for the moon-god (Nanna/Sin), a star for Inanna/Ishtar (the planet Venus), seven dots or small stars for the constellation Pleiades (of which seven are readily visible, or 'Seven Sisters')...."

Civilizations of the Ancient Near East, Vol. III,
ed. Jack M. Sasson, (New York), p. 1841.

"...the Ka'aba was dedicated to al-Llah, the High God of the pagan Arabs, despite the presiding effigy of Hubal. By the beginning of the seventh century, al-Llah had become more important than before in the religious life many of

the Arabs. Many primitive religions develop a
belief in a High God, who is sometimes called the
Sky God... but they also carried on worshipping
the other gods, who remained deeply important to
them."

Karen Armstrong, *Muhammad*, (New York: San
Francisco, 1992), p. 69.

"The cult of a deity termed simply "the god"
(al-ilah) was known throughout southern Syria and
northern Arabia in the days before Islam –
Muhammad's father was named 'Abd Allah'
("Servant of Allah") – and was obviously of
central importance in Mecca, where the building
called the Ka'bah was indisputably his house.
Indeed, the Muslims shahadah attest to precisely
that point: the Quraysh, the paramount tribe of
Mecca, were being called on by Muhammad to
repudiate the very existence of all the other gods
save this one. It seems equally certain that Allah
was not merely a god in Mecca but was widely
regarded as the "high god", the chief and head of
the Meccan pantheon, whether this was the result,
as has been argued, of a natural progression
toward henotheism or of the growing influence of
Jews and Christians in the Arabian Peninsula....
Thus Allah was neither an unknown nor an
unimportant deity to the Quraysh when
Muhammad began preaching his worship at
Mecca."

The Oxford Encyclopedia of the Modern Islamic
World, ed. John L. Esposito, (New York, 1995),
pp. 76-77.

"The religion of the Arabs, as well as their political life, was on a thoroughly primitive level.... In particular the Semites regarded trees, caves, springs, and large stones as being inhabited by spirits; like the Black Stone of Islam in a corner of the Ka'bah at Mecca, in Petra and other places in Arabia stones were venerated also.... Every tribe worshipped its own god, but also recognized the power of other tribal gods in their own sphere.... Three goddesses in particular had elevated themselves above the circle of the inferior demons. The goddess of fate, al-Manat, corresponding to the Tyche Soteira of the Greeks, though known in Mecca, was worshipped chiefly among the neighboring Bedouin tribes of the Hudhayl. Allat – "the Goddess", who is Taif was called ar-Rabbah, "the Lady", and whom Herodotus equates with Urania – corresponded to the great mother of the gods, Astarte of the northern Semites; al-'Uzza, "the Mightiest", worshipped in the planet Venus, was merely a variant form.... In addition to all these gods and goddesses, the Arabs, like many other primitive peoples, believed in a God who was creator of the world, Allah, whom the Arabs did not, as has often been thought, owe to the Jews and Christians.... The more the significance of the cult declined, the greater became the value of a general religious temper associated with Allah. Among the Meccans he was already coming to take the place of the old moon-god Hubal as the lord of the Ka'bah.... Allah was actually the guardian of contracts, though at first they were still settled at a special ritual locality and so subordinate to the

supervision of an idol. In particular he was
regarded as the guardian of the alien guest, though
consideration for him still lagged behind duty to
one's kinsman."

History of the Islamic Peoples, Carl
Brockelmann, (New York), pp. 8-10.

"The Romans and Abyssinians were
identified with Christianity. Whole tribes and
districts held up the banner of Judaism and waged
war in its propagation. The Persian power was the
exponent of the fire-worship; and the Arabs in
general were devoted to that native idolatry which
had its center in the national sanctuary of the
Kaaba.... The religion most widely prevalent in
Arabia, when Mohammed began his life, was a
species of heathenism of idol-worship, which had
its local center in Mecca and its temple....
According to a theory held by many, this temple
had been sourceally connected with the ancient
worship of the sun, moon and stars, and its
circumambulation by the worshippers had a
symbolical reference to the rotation of the
heavenly bodies. Within its precincts and in its
neighborhood there were found many idols, such
as Hobal, Lat, Ozza, Manah, Wadd, Sawa,
Yaghut, Nasr, Isaf, Naila, etc. A black stone in the
temple was was regarded with superstitious awe as
eminently sacred.... The attempt of the
Mussulmans to derive it direct from a stone altar
or pillar, erected by Abraham and his son Ismael,
in that identical locality, is altogether unsupported
by history, and, in fact, flagrantly contrary to the
biblical record of the life of Abraham and his son.

The pagan character of the temple is sufficiently marked by the statement of Mohammedan writers that before its purification by their Prophet, it contained no less than 360 idols, as many as there were days of the year; and that on its walls were painted the figures of angels, prophets, saints, including those of Abraham and Ismael, and even of the Virgin Mary with her infant Son.... Mohammed, with great practical insight and shrewdness, seized on this advantage and retained the heathen shrine of his native city as the local center of Islam. He sanctioned it by his own example as a place of religious pilgrimage for all his followers."

Mohammed and Mohammedanism, S. W. Koelle, (London, 1889), p. 17-19

"According to D. Nielsen, the starting point of the religion of the Semitic nomads was marked by the astral triad, Sun-Moon-Venus, the moon being more important for the nomads and the sun more important for the settled tribes."

Studies on Islam, trans., ed. Merlin L. Swartz, (New York, Oxford, 1981), p.7.

"One detail which already impressed the Greek authors was the role played by sacred stones.... The material object is not venerated for itself but rather as the dwelling of either a person being (god, spirit) or a force."

Studies on Islam, ibid., p. 8.

"The final divinity to be considered is Allah who was recognized before Islam as god, and if not as the only god at least as a supreme god. The Quran makes it quite clear that he was recognized at Mecca, though belief in him was certainly more widespread.... How is this to be explained? Earlier scholars attributed the diffusion of this belief solely to Christian and Judaic influences. But now a growing number of authors maintain that this idea had older roots in Arabia.... If, therefore, Allah is indigenous to Arabia, one must ask further: Are there indications of a nomadic source? I think there are, based on a comparison of the beliefs of the nomads in central and northern Asia with those of northeastern Africa. Like the supreme being of many other nomads, Allah is a god of the sky and dispenser of rain."

Studies on Islam, ibid., p. 12.

"The ibex (wa'al) still inhabits South Arabia and in Sabean times represented the moon god. Dr. Albert Jamme believes it was of religious significance to the ancient Sabeans that the curved ibex horn held sideways resembled the first quarter of the moon."

Qataban and Sheba: Exploring the Ancient Kingdoms on the Biblical Spice Routes of Arabia, Wendell Phillips, (New York, 1955), p. 64.

"The first pre-Islamic inscription discovered in Dhofar Province, Oman, this bronze plaque, deciphered by Dr. Albert Jamme, dates from about the second century A.D. and gives the name of the

Hadramaut moon god Sin and the name
Sumhuram, a long-lost city…. The moon was the
chief deity of all the early South Arabian
kingdoms – particularly fitting in that region
where the soft light of the moon brought the rest
and cool winds of night as a relief from the
blinding sun and scorching heat of day.

"In contrast to most of the old religions with
which we are familiar, the moon god is male,
while the sun god is his consort, a female. The
third god of importance is their child, the male
morning star, which we know as the planet
Venus….

"The spice route riches brought them a
standard of luxurious living inconceivable to the
poverty-stricken South Arabian bedouins of today.
Like nearly all Semitic peoples they worshipped
the moon, the sun, and the morning star. The chief
god, the moon, was a male deity symbolized by
the bull, and we found many carved bulls' heads,
with drains for the blood of sacrificed animals."

*Qataban and Sheba: Exploring the Ancient
Kingdoms on the Biblical Spice Routes of
Arabia*, ibid. p. 227.

"Arabia in Muhammad's time was
polytheistic in its conception of the cosmos and
tribal in its social structure. Each tribe had its own
god(s) and goddess(es), which were manifest in
the forms of idols, stones, trees, or stars in the
sky."

*Islamic Studies, A History of Religions
Approach*, 2nd Ed., Richard C. Martin,
(NewJersey), p. 96.

"II. The Religion of the Pre-Islamic Arabs

"The life of the pre-Islamic Arabs, especially in the Hijaz, depended on trade and they made a trade of their religion as well. About four hundred years before the birth of Muhammad one Amr bin Lahyo bin Harath bin Amr ul-Qais bin Thalaba bin Azd bin Khalan bin Babalyun bin Saba, a descendant of Qahtan and king of Hijaz, had put an idol called Habal on the roof of the Kaba. This was one of the chief deities of the Quraish before Islam. It is said that there were altogether three hundred and sixty idols in and about the Kaba and that each tribe had its own deity.... The shapes and figures of the idols were also made according to the fancy of the worshippers. Thus Wadd was shaped like a man, Naila like a woman, so was Suwa. Yaghuth was made in the shape of a lion, Yauq like a horse and Nasr like a vulture.... Besides Hodal, there was another idol called Shams placed on the roof of the Kaba.... The blood of the sacrifical animals brought by the pilgrims was offered to the deities in the Kaba and sometimes even human beings were sacrificed and offered to the god.... Besides idol-worship, they also worshipped the stars, the sun and the moon."

Muhammad the Holy Prophet, Hafiz Ghulam
Sarwar (Pakistan), p. 18-19.

"The Bedouin do not seem to have had much time for religion. They were realists, without a great deal of imagination. They believed the land was peopled by spirits, the jinns, who were often invisible but appeared also in animal form. The dead were thought to live on in a dim and ghostly state. Offerings were made to them and stelae and cairns of stones erected on their graves. Certain trees and stones (especially meteorites and those shaped to resemble human forms) housed spirits and divinities. Divinities dwelt in the sky and some were actually stars. Some were thought to be ancient sages made divine. The list of these divine beings, and above all the importance with which each was regarded, varied from one tribe to the next; but the chief of them were to be found all over the peninsula. This was especially true of Allah, 'the God, the Divinity', the personification of the divine world in its highest form, creator of the universe and keeper of sworn oaths. In the Hejaz three goddesses had pride of place as the 'daughters of Allah'. The first of these was Allat, mentioned by Herodotus under the name of Alilat. Her name means simply 'the goddess', and she may have stood for one aspect of Venus, the morning star, although hellenized Arabs identified her with Athene. Next came Uzza, 'the all-powerful'; whom other sources identify with Venus. The third was Manat, the goddess of fate, who held the shears which cut the thread of life and who was worshipped in a shrine on the seashore. The great god of Mecca was Hubal, an idol made of red cornelian.... Homage was paid to the divinity with offerings and the sacrifice of

animals and perhaps, occasionally, of human
beings. Certain sanctuaries were the object of
pilgrimage (hajj) at which a variety of rituals were
performed, consisting notably of ceremonial
processions around the sacred object. Certain
prohibitions had to be observed during these
rituals, such as in many cases abstention from
sexual relations. Magic was common. People
feared the evil eye and protected themselves with
amulets."

Mohammed, Maxine Rodinson, (New York), pp.
16-17.

"These and many other verses show clearly
that the existence of a god called Allah and even
his highest position among the divinities was
known and acknowledged in Jahiliyyah, but He
was, after all, but one of the gods.... Was the
Koranic concept of Allah a continuation of the
pre-Islamic one, or did the former represent a
complete break with the latter? Were there some
essential – not accidental – ties between the two
concepts signified by one and the same name? Or
was it a simple matter of a common word used for
two different objects?

"In order to be able to give a satisfactory
answer to these initial questions, we will do well
to remember the fact that, when the Koran began
to use this name, there immediately arose serious
debates among the Arabs of Mecca. The Koranic
usage of the word provoked stormy discussions
over the nature of this God between the Muslims

and the Kafirs, as is most eloquently attested by
the Koran itself.

"What does this mean from the semantical
point of view? What are the implications of the
fact that the name of Allah was not only known to
both parties but was actually used by both parties
in their discussion with each other? The very fact
that the name of Allah was common to both the
pagan Arabs and the Muslims, particularly the fact
that it gave rise to much heated discussion about
the concept of God, would seem to suggest
conclusively that there was some common ground
of understanding between the two parties.
Otherwise there could have been neither debate
nor discussion at all. And when the Prophet
addressed his adversaries in the name of Allah, he
did so simply and solely because he knew that this
name meant something – and something important
– to their minds too. If this were not so, his
activity would have been quite pointless in this
respect.

"As regards the 'basic' meaning of Allah,
…In pre-Islamic times each tribe, as a rule, had its
own local god or divinity known by a proper
name. So, at first, each tribe may have meant its
own local divinity when it used an expression
equivalent in meaning to 'the God'; this is quite
probable. But the very fact that people began to
designate their own local divinity by the abstract
form of 'the God' must have paved the way for the
growth of an abstract notion of God without any
localizing qualification and then, following this,

for a belief in the supreme God common to all the tribes. We meet with similar instances all over the world.

"Before the name [Allah] came into Islam, it had already long been part of the pre-Islamic system, and a considerably important part, too... the pagan concept of Allah, which is purely Arabian – the case in which we see the pre-Islamic Arabs themselves talking about 'Allah' as they understood the word in their own peculiar way."

God and Man in the Koran, Toshihiko Izutsu, (Tokyo, 1964), pp. 95-99, 103-104.

IS THE GOD OF ISLAM A TRUE OR FALSE GOD?

Every religion claims to worship the "True" God, gods or goddesses. After all, what religion would say that it worships a *false* god? Either one religion is right and the others are false, or they are all false. But they cannot all be right.

Like any other religion, Islam claims to worship the "true" God. The deity of Islam has been given ninety-nine names but is known primarily by the title "Allah." Logically speaking, the burden of proof is on the Muslims. They must prove that "Allah" is the "true" god.

The first problem we face is that modern Muslims never bother to prove that "Allah" is "God." They simply assert that this is true. Thus they end up arguing in a circle by assuming what they have yet to prove. To chant "Allah is Great" is not the same thing as proving that he is God.

They also commit the fallacy of assuming that if they attack the Triune God of Christianity, Allah wins by default. But both gods could be false.

The second problem is that the attributes of Allah as found in the Qur'an reveal that he is not "God" in the classical Judeo-Christian sense.

1. He is a god of deceit and trickery instead of a God of Truth (Surah 3:54). As such, he is fickle and cannot be trusted.

2. He commands men to sin (Surah 17:16) and wills them to unbelief (Surah 7:89) and then he punishes them for it.

3. In Surahs 4:171 and 5:116, he said that the Trinity was composed of the Father, the Mother, and the Son. This shows that he is an ignorant god.

4. His "paradise" is a corrupt place filled with drunkenness and sexual orgies with houries and young men (Surahs 2:25; 4:57; 47:15; 56:15-23).

5. His speech is filled with grammatical errors such as confusing gender and number in the same sentence (Surahs 7:160; 2:17; 42:17, etc.).

6. He contradicted himself. For example, Surah 41:5-9 says there were eight days of creation, while Surah 7:54 says there were only six days.

7. He made scientific errors such as the sun setting in a muddy pond (Surah 18:86) or people turning into apes (Surah 2:65).

8. He made historical errors such as having the Samaritans exist before there was a Samaria. (Surah 20:85, 87, 95).

9. He was mistaken when he said that he had sent down the Qur'an in pure Arabic (Surahs 12:2; 13:37; 41:44; 43:7). It has many foreign words.

10. He would say one thing and then turn around and abrogate it (Surahs 2:106; 16:101).

Since some liberal Muslims claim that their "Allah" is the same God found in the Bible, it is important to review the facts. "Allah" is not the God of the Bible for the following reasons:

1. He is not the holy Trinity of Father, Son, and Holy Spirit.

2. He never became incarnate and died for our sins on the cross.

3. He is not a savior.

4. We must save ourselves by our own good works.

5. He is Antichrist according to I John 2:22-23.

"This is the antichrist, the one who denies the Father and the Son. Whoever denies the Son does not have the Father; the one who confesses the Son has the Father also."

Since Islam says that Jesus was not the Son of Allah and Allah is not his Father, it does not take Ph.D. to figure out that Allah is not the God of the Bible.

6. "Allah" was the father of Al-Lat, Al-Uzza and Manat. The "daughters of Allah" are referred to in the Qur'an in the famous "Satanic Verses" (Surah 53:9-21).

7. Allah was originally the moon god who was married to the sun goddess. The stars were their offspring.

8. Muhammad's father, Abdullah, lived and died as a pagan and yet Allah was part of his name, "Abdullah," because it referred to a pagan god.

9. The rituals associated with the worship of the pagan god Allah were adopted by Muhammad as an essential part of Islam. This especially applies to praying toward Mecca, the Pilgrimage (HAJJ) to Mecca, the Fast of Ramadan, and other essential rituals of Islam.

10. Islam has adopted the name, the rituals, and the crescent moon symbol of the moon-god. But it now denies that he has a wife or daughters. Thus Allah remains the same pagan deity minus his wife and daughters.

CONCLUSION

Given these facts, it is clear that only the ignorant, the naïve or the deceived fanatic would say that the Allah of the Qur'an is the same triune God revealed in the Bible and worshipped by Christians.

CHAPTER TWO

WHO WAS MUHAMMAD?

As pointed out by Ibn Warraq in his landmark work, *The Quest for the Historical Muhammad*, the "Muhammad" of faith and religion is *not* the Muhammad of fact and history. Modern Muslims have a legendary and mythological view of the character and life of Muhammad that is in direct contradiction of *all* the historical accounts.

In my debate with the Muslim apologist, Shabir Ally, (to obtain a copy, call 1-800-41-TRUTH), he argued that Muhammad was a prophet because, on one occasion, he ordered his entire caravan to stop while a dog gave birth to a litter of puppies. He offered no historical evidence to back up this tender story.

I pointed out that the story, even if it were true, did not logically prove that Muhammad was a prophet. Lots of people are kind to animals. But, more to the point, the historical record is 100% clear that Muhammad ordered that all dogs be killed!

> Umar: Allah's Apostle ordered that the dogs should be killed.

Bukhari vol. IV, no. 540 Narrated Abdullah bib

The tender story of Muhammad holding up his caravan for a dog giving birth goes against his edict that all dogs should be killed. Even today, dogs as pets are forbidden by Islamic law. The first thing the Ayatollah did after taking over Iran was to kill all the dogs in the country!

The example above highlights the problem. The Muhammad of myth and legend has so ingrained itself into the mindset of modern Muslims that, even when you quote the Qur'an or the Hadith, they will refuse to listen.

A PERFECT AND SINLESS MUHAMMAD

One classic example of this bias is the Muslim doctrine that Muhammad was both perfect and sinless. When I stated in my lecture at the University of Texas, that Muhammad was *not* sinless, the Muslims in the audience went crazy. (To obtain a copy of this video, call 1-800-41-TRUTH).

Can Muslims produce any passages from the Qur'an or the Hadith that state that Muhammad was sinless? No. I have asked for such passages for over twenty years and no Muslim has been able to find one.

When I quoted passages from the Qur'an (Surah 40:55; 48:1-2, etc.) that clearly state that Allah commanded Muhammad to repent of his sins or that Allah had forgiven him of his sins, they ignored them. When I quoted from the Hadith (Bukhari, vol. I., nos. 19, 711, 781) where Muhammad said that he asked for forgiveness for his sins many times a day, they still would not give up their belief that Muhammad was perfect. They believe it because, well, they just believe it! Even their own sacred books cannot open their minds to the real Muhammad.

THE BURDEN OF PROOF

Muslim theologians begin by assuming that their beliefs are true. Thus they assume that they do not have to prove anything, but they have it backwards. They have the burden of proof to demonstrate that Muhammad was a true prophet and not just another false prophet.

There are only four logical possibilities.

1. He was who he claimed to be: a prophet and an apostle,

2. He was a liar: he knew he was not a prophet but for money, sex and power, he claimed to be one,

3. He was mentally ill: if he were alive today he would be institutionalized as criminally insane, or...

4. He was a mentally ill liar: he had delusions of grandeur and he lied when it suited his purposes.

WHERE'S THE BEEF?

One obvious question that comes to mind about Islam is, "Why did the 7th century Arabs accept Muhammad as a prophet?" There were no biblical or pagan prophecies that foretold his coming. He was semi-illiterate and only of average intelligence. Why did they follow him?"

The natural blood lust of the 7th century Arab was no doubt stirred by Muhammad's call to kill, rape and plunder in the name of Allah. Their quest for more slaves was no doubt satisfied by Muhammad's proclaiming "open season"

on all non-Muslims. But these things cannot explain
everything.

PRE-ISLAMIC ARABIA

The truth is found in pre-Islamic Arabia. The pagan
Arabs, like many other barbaric peoples, believed in
shamans (kahin) or what we call today "witch doctors" or
"medicine men". These "prophets" were revered as having
magical powers over the forces of nature and over the
spirits that inhabited trees, rocks, ponds and streams.

Muhammad presented himself to the pagan Arabs as a
shaman. This is clear from both the Qur'an and the Hadith.
As documented in my book, *Islamic Invasion*, Muhammad
claimed to control the jinn; i.e., the spirits who lived in the
trees, rocks, ponds and streams. In the Hadith, Muhammad
is pictured as being in control of the forces of nature, and
he could supposedly make it rain or cause a drought by his
prayers.

PROOF #1—THE SEAL OF PROPHETHOOD

The pagan Arabs looked for certain physical defects on
the body as a sign of prophethood. They believed that a
"seal" of prophethood would be found on the body of a
shaman or prophet. This "seal" was a large hairy mole on
the back of the shaman just below the neck.

Just like a lump of wax seals a letter, the gods would
place a lump of flesh on the back of someone called to be a
shaman. What the pagan Arabs wanted to know was
whether or not Muhammad had a large hairy mole on his
back. Did he have the "Seal" of prophethood?

In the Qur'an we read these words in Surah 33:40:

"Muhammad is not the father of any of your
men, but he is the apostle of Allah, and has the
Seal of the prophets: and Allah has full knowledge
of all things."

What is the identity of this "Seal of the prophets" and
what is its significance? There are two ways of answering
these questions. If you ask a modern Muslim what this
"Seal" was all about, the answer would depend on whether
you were talking to a Sunni or a Shi'ite Muslim.

Sunni Muslims believe that Muhammad was the last of
the prophets; i.e., there will be no prophets after him. (See
Yusuf Ali's comment in his translation of the Qur'an, n.
3731, pg. 1119, as an example of how the Sunnis interpret
the significance of the "Seal".)

The Shi'ites believe in a succession of prophets. This
is why the Ayatollahs have so much power in Iran. The
Sunnis and Shi'ites fight and kill each other over the issue
of future prophets.

But we are not asking about future prophets. Instead,
we are asking a *historical* question: *"What did the early
Muslims believe concerning the 'Seal of the prophets?'"* In
fact, we are asking: *"What did the most trusted and revered
companions, historians, and theologians say about this
'Seal' of the prophets mentioned in the Qur'an?"*

The Hadith scholars were unanimous in their
interpretation of the identity and significance of the "Seal
of the prophets" found in Surah 33:40. The greatest of all
Hadith scholars, al-Bukhari, tells us:

Narrated As-Sa'ib bin Yazid: I stood behind
him (i.e., Muhammad) and saw the seal of

Prophethood between his shoulders, and it was like the "Zir-al-Hijla" (meaning the button of a small tent, but some say "egg of a partridge") (vol. 1:189; 4:741).

The second greatest work on the Hadith is, without a doubt, the Sahih Muslim Hadith. It records the following:

THE FACT PERTAINING TO THE SEAL OF HIS PROPHETHOOD, ITS CHARACTER- ISTIC FEATURE, AND ITS LOCATION ON HIS BODY.

Jabir b. Sammura reported: I saw the seal on his back as it were a pigeon's egg. This Hadith has been narrated on the authority of Simal with the same chain of transmitters. Abdullah b. Sarjis reported: I went in after him and saw the Seal of Prophethood between his shoulders on the left side of his shoulder having spots on it like moles (vol. IV, CMLXXIX, p. 1251).

The early Muslim scholars clearly held to the same view of the seal. It was a large hairy mole on Muhammad's back which signified that he was a prophet.

A mole of an unusual size on the Prophet's back which is said to have been the divine seal which, according to the predictions of the Scriptures, marked Muhammad as the "Seal of the Prophets" (Khatimu 'n-Nabiyin).

It was the size of the knob of the bridal canopy. Others say it was even the size of a closed fist (Mishkatu 'I-Masabih, book iii, ch. 7).

It was a piece of flesh, very brilliant in appearance, and according to some traditions it

had secretly inscribed within it "Allah is one and
has no associate" (Shaikh 'Abdu 'I-Haqq).

Muhammad said to Abu Ramsa, "Come hither
and touch my back." Which he did, drawing his
fingers over the prophetical seal, and behold!
There was a collection of hairs upon the spot.
When Abu Ramsa offered to remove it,
Muhammad said, "The Physician thereof is He
who placed it where it is" (Muir, new edition, p.
542).

The Dictionary of Islam interprets the "Seal of
Prophecy" as:

This, says one, was a protuberance on the
Prophet's back of the size and appearance of a
pigeon's egg. It is said to have been the divine seal
which, according to the predictions of the
Scriptures, marked Muhammad as the last of the
Prophets.... From the traditions, it would seem to
have been nothing more than a mole of unusual
size (p. 389).

Ali Tabari, one of the most respected early
apologists for Islam, interpreted the "seal of the
Prophets" as a mole on Muhammad's back. He
desperately tried to find some biblical prophecy
that would predict such a physical sign. He seized
upon Isaiah 9:6 as a prophecy of Muhammad. He
took the phrase "... and the government shall be
upon his shoulders ..." and interpreted it as a
prophecy concerning moles! During the debate he
claimed, "Unto us a child is born and unto us a
child is given, whose government is on his
shoulder" (Isaiah 9:6). He means by that, "His

prophecy is on his shoulder." In the Hebrew, it is
said: "The sign of prophecy is on his shoulder."
This is what the Muslims call "the sign of
prophecy." This is therefore a clear allusion to the
portraiture (i.e., physical characteristics) of the
prophet - may Allah bless and save him - and a
reference to his face and his moles.

(N. A. Newman, Early Christian- Muslim
Dialogue, [I.B.R.I.: Hatfield, PA, 1994] p. 628)

We could go on with many more references from early
Muslim theologians and historians, but these citations are
sufficient to prove the "seal of prophecy" referred to in
Surah 33:40 was a large hairy mole on Muhammad's back.
While such physical defects are often looked upon by
pagans as a mystical sign, nowhere in the Bible are such
things ever considered a sign of inspiration. Indeed, Lev.
21:16-24 *excludes* from holy service anyone who had a
physical defect!

As to Isaiah 9:6, it refers to the Messiah whose title is
"Mighty God". Obviously, the word "government" does
not mean a mole. I have not found a single Hebrew scholar
who views the word "government" as meaning mole.

The pagan Arabs were looking for a prophet who had a
physical deformity like a large mole or tumor on his back.
Muhammad had such a mole. Thus he was a pagan shaman.
That is why he won over so many pagan Arabs.

PROOF #2—EPILEPTIC SEIZURES

Another religious tradition among pagan Arabs was
that someone who fell down and had a seizure was either
possessed by the jinn (i.e., demons) or inspired by the gods

or God. Once again, brain seizures, like physical deformities, are not a part of the biblical tradition.

Liberals view the medical diagnosis that Muhammad was an epileptic and that his seizures played a major role in pagan Arabs accepting him as a prophet, as "politically incorrect". But the historical and medical evidence is drawn from authentic Muslim sacred writings. *The Dictionary of Islam* (p.393) explains,

> He (i.e. Muhammad) suffered from hallucinations of his senses, and to finish his sufferings, he several times contemplated suicide by throwing himself down from a precipice. His friends were alarmed at his state of mind. Some considered it as eccentricities of a poetical genius; others thought that he was a *kahin*, or soothsayer; but the majority took a *less* charitable view (See Surah lxix.40, xx.5), and declared that he was insane; and, as madness and melancholy are ascribed to supernatural influence in the East, they said that he was in the power of Satan and his agents, the jinn. They called in exorcists; and he himself doubted the soundness of his mind. "I hear a sound," he said to his wife, "and I see a light. I am afraid there are jinn in me."
>
> And on another occasion he said, "I am afraid that I am a *kahin*."
>
> According to unimpeachably authentic hadiths found in Bukhari, Muhammad heard ringing in his ears; his heart beat rapidly; his face turned red; his breathing labored; he would fall to the ground or lie down; he would shake; his eyes would open wide; his lips tremble; spit drooled

from the corners of his mouth; he would sweat
profusely; he saw and heard things no one else
ever saw or heard; he would sometimes make a
snoring noise like that of a camel; and he would be
covered with a sheet.

> vol I, nos. 1, 2, 3, 4; vol. II, nos. chap. 16 (pg. 354),
> 544; vol. III, nos. 17, 829; vol. IV, nos. 95, 438, 458,
> 461; vol. V, nos. 170, 462, 618, 659; vol. VI, nos. 447,
> 448, 468, 478, 481, 508.

In *McClintock and Strong's Encyclopedia* (vol. 6, pg.
406), we read the following:

Muhammad was endowed with a nervous
constitution and a lively imagination. It was not at
all unnatural for him to come after a time to regard
himself as actually called of God to build up his
people in a new faith.

Muhammad, as we gather from the oldest and
most trust-worthy narratives, was an epileptic, and
as such, was considered to be possessed of evil
spirits. At first, he believed the sayings, but
gradually he came to the conclusion, confirmed by
his friends, that demons had no power over so
pure and pious a man as he was, and he conceived
the idea that he was not controlled by evil spirits,
but that he was visited by angels whom he,
disposed to hallucinations, a vision, an audition,
afflicted with the morbid state of the body and
mind, saw in dreams. Or even while awake, he
conceived he saw. What seemed to him good and
true after such epileptic attacks, he esteemed
revelation in which he, at least in the first stage of
his pathetic course, firmly believed and which
imparted to his pensive, variable character, the

necessary courage and endurance to brave all mortifications and perils.

Whenever any scholar brings up the medical evidence that proves that Muhammad had the classic symptoms of epilepsy, the liberals object that to say this is insensitive. But the evidence, like a granite rock, is unmoved by crying and hand wringing.

This medical evidence has been gathered and explained by modern science and psychiatry. One recent example is the book, *Life Alert* (Winepress Pub. 2002), by Dr. Korkut, M.D. His analysis of the medical evidence cannot be overthrown simply because the feelings of Muslims are offended. He certifies that Muhammad suffered from two neurological deficiencies: *hydrocephalus* and *epilepsy*. If you wish to view his evidence, call 1-800-41-TRUTH and order it.

PROOF #3—NO PREDICTIONS OF HIS COMING

Muslim theologians accept the fact that the Hebrew Scriptures predicted the coming of the Messiah and that Jesus was the one who fulfilled those prophecies. They are also keenly aware that the Qur'an (in Surahs 7 and 61) claims that the Bible predicted the coming of Muhammad. Thus there has been a desperate attempt to find anything by any stretch of the imagination that could possibly be used as a prediction of the coming of Muhammad. This has driven the Muslims to the most absurd interpretation of biblical texts and words. So absurd that one wonders how any sane person would have the gall to give them.

The Muslim arguments fall into four groups. The first is an argument drawn from the erroneous idea that Ishmael was the father of the Arabs. The second argument is geographical. The third focuses on particular words and the fourth on specific biblical texts.

In order for these arguments to work, the text must have all the following elements:

- a prediction of the coming of a prophet,
- this prophet must be an Arab,
- and his name must be Muhammad.

If the passage does not refer to an Arab prophet named Muhammad, then it is useless.

1. *The Ishmaelite Arguments*

Moses, in Deut. 18:18, predicted that YHWH would send a prophet in the future who would be like Moses. The New Testament clearly teaches that Jesus was this long awaited prophet. But most Muslim apologists have claimed that Muhammad was the one who fulfilled Deut. 18:18. Who is right?

The prophecy in Deut. 18 states that the coming prophet would come from Moses' brethren; i.e., the Jews. Since the Arabs descend from Ham and the Jews from Shem, the Arabs are not Jews. How can a prophecy concerning a coming *Jewish* prophet be fulfilled by a *gentile* Arab called Muhammad?

This is why the myth that Ishmael was the father of the Arabs was created out of thin air. The Bible nowhere states that the Arabs are the children of Abraham through Ishmael. No pre-Islamic genealogy kept by Arab tribes mentions Ishmael as their father.

In a later chapter, we will demonstrate that Ishmael was not the father of the Arab people. Thus Muhammad cannot be the Jewish prophet predicted in Deut. 18 because he was not a Jew.

This immediately throws out all arguments based on references to Ishmael or his descendents. Badawi's attempt to argue from such words as Paran, Ke'dar, Sa'ir, etc. falls to the ground.

2. *The Geographical Arguments*

Muslim apologists such a Deedat, Badawi and Shabir have assumed that if they can find in the Bible a passing reference to some place in Arabia, then this would automatically prove that Muhammad was in the Bible. Of course, this is logically absurd!

Since the Bible refers to many ancient cities and countries, even if there were a reference to Mecca or Arabia, this would not logically prove anything. Do the biblical references to Babylon prove that the coming prophet would be a Babylonian? Of course not!

The key is to interpret a passage in terms of its literary genre and its context. If the passage cited is a historical narrative with no apocalyptic elements, then it cannot be used to predict the coming of anyone.

In addition to being based on a logical fallacy, the geographical arguments are not factual. The words that are used to link the Bible to Mecca or to Arabia are erroneous.

The Bible refers to a place called "Baca" in Ps. 84:4-6. How do Muslims go from Baca to Mecca? They chant, "Baca, Maca, Mecca." They replace the "B" with a "M" and the "a" with an "e" and move from Baca to Mecca.

There are several problems with this argument. First, there is no linguistic justification for arbitrarily switching Hebrew letters. Second, there is no Hebrew manuscript that changes the spelling. Third, simply chanting a phonic fallacy cannot change the manuscript evidence. Fourth, in Ps. 84, Baca was a valley in Northern Israel that was on the pilgrim pathway to Mt. Zion, a symbol for worship at the temple in Jerusalem.

3. *Specific words*

a. The attempt to twist the word, Teman, in Hab. 3:3 into a reference to Muhammad's flight to Medina goes beyond belief. If you check all the other references to Teman, it is a place of ignorance and divine judgment (Ezk. 25:13; Jer. 49:7, 20; Amos 1:12, etc.).

b. Perhaps the silliest arguments revolve around the attempt to configure the name "Muhammad" from such words as Amen, Ahmed, etc. One of the weakest is from Song of Solomon 5:16 where they attempt to twist the Hebrew word for praise into the Arabic word, Muhammad. That they arbitrarily jump from one language to another language does not seem to dawn on them.

c. The same can be said of pointing to passages where the word "sword" appears (Ps. 45:2-5), or the person rode on a camel (Isa. 21:7). Since swords were popular in those days and everyone rode on camels, it is insane to think that such references have to do with a pagan Arab prophet of the moon-god Allah.

4. *Specific Passages*

a. In John 16, Jesus predicted the coming of the Holy Spirit as the Comforter who would indwell the people of

God forever yet Muslims attempt to depict Muhammad as the divine Comforter predicted by Jesus.

The main problem with their argument is their ignorance of the Greek New Testament. They often misspell parakletos as perilytos. They have no right to alter the Greek text to suit their claim.

Also, the Holy Spirit came upon the Church at Pentecost and the claim that a pagan prophet by the name of Muhammad fulfilled the prophecy seven centuries later is without merit. Since Muhammad died, how, pray tell, does he indwell the hearts of the followers of Jesus forever?

b. The attempt of Muslim apologists to take passages that describe *God* coming in judgment with ten thousand angels (ex.: Deut. 33:1-3) and arbitrarily apply them to Muhammad going into battle with ten thousand thieves and murderers is blasphemous to say the least. Muhammad was not God and the raping, murdering, looting hordes who followed him were more like demons than angels.

CONCLUSION

The burden of proof is on the Muslims to demonstrate by valid arguments that Muhammad was not criminally insane, but a prophet. They have tried, but failed to fulfill their burden.

CHAPTER THREE

WHAT IS THE QUR'AN?

When you pick up a copy of the Qur'an, several questions should immediately come to you mind:

Who?	Authorship
What?	Literary Nature
Where?	Place of Origin
When?	Time of Writing
How?	Medium of Transmission
Why?	Justification of Need

These questions are good and necessary. But how can we find answers to them? Two different approaches to answering these questions exist:

The Muslim approach depends upon secondary sources that were put together generations after Muhammad died. The Sunna and the Hadith supply the Muslim with the official answers to these questions. Thus while the Qur'an does not answer the questions above, the Hadith does.

Note: Muslims are guilty of circular reasoning at this point: They prove the Qur'an by the Hadith, and then prove the Hadith by the Qur'an!

The secular approach focuses on the issue of primary sources. It questions the veracity of the Traditions as well as the veracity of the Qur'an. It does not want material written in the ninth or tenth century telling them what was written in the seventh century. They want actual material from the seventh and eighth century. The failure of the Muslims to come up with anything in this regard has great implications.

PART 1: THE MUSLIM APPROACH

The Hadith is sometimes called the "second inspiration" with the Qur'an being the first inspiration. The Hadith claims to be the record of Muhammad's exposition and application of the Qur'an, biographical material on Muhammad, and the history of the writing, collection, and composition of the text of the Qur'an (Bukhari VI:564).

The authority and authenticity of the Qur'an depends entirely upon the integrity and teachings of the Hadith. In other words, the Qur'an is valid only if the Hadith is true. If it is false, then the Qur'an is automatically false.

The Integrity of Muhammad

The integrity of Muhammad is all-important. He was either who he claimed to be, a liar or a nut case (mentally insane or demon possessed). This is why the Traditions went to such great lengths to create a model of Muhammad that depicts him as a "super man" as well as a prophet. What do we find in the Hadith?

1. Muhammad's credentials for prophethood are unacceptable. The two prominent Hadithic "proofs" of his prophethood came from pagan ideas of what a shaman would look like and the manner in which he would be inspired.

A.   The Hadith explains that when the Qur'an refers to the seal of prophethood being upon Muhammad (Surah 33:40), the seal was a large hairy mole on his back. This is found in both Bukhari (I:189; IV:741) and Muslim (IV:5790, 5793). This mole was the physical proof that Muhammad was a prophet according to Tabari and other later Muslim authorities. They even claimed that the mole was a fulfillment of such Scriptures as Isaiah 9:6. We cannot accept this as proof. While such ideas can be found in pagan traditions from many primitive cultures, it is not a part of the religion of Abraham, the prophets, the Apostles, or of Jesus.

B.   Both the Bukhari and Muslim Hadiths describe what happened to Muhammad when inspiration came upon him. He heard ringing in his ears, fell to the ground, turned red, sweated profusely, made moaning sounds, spit drooled from his mouth, etc. While ancient pagans placed a great deal of importance on such things, they were never a part of the biblical tradition.

2. He failed a direct test of his claim to prophethood. He was asked to explain why a child looks like one parent as opposed to looking like the other. He claimed that Gabriel came and gave the inspired answer. See Bukhari IV:546. So, we are dealing with revelation and not just his personal opinion. He said that the child will look like whichever parent reaches his or her sexual climax first. The study of genetics and DNA forever disproves this idea.

3. He believed in magic, the evil eye, amulets, omens,
    spells, etc. He was superstitious about many things
    and made up weird rules about bathroom duties
    (Bukhari I:144; IV:110, 111; VII:636, 649, 650; and
    Muslim I:458; III:5424, 5427). He was afraid
    whenever a strong wind blew (Bukhari II:144), and
    of eclipses (Bukhari II:167).

While this is bad enough, the Hadith tells us that
Muhammad was at times under magical spells; i.e.,
bewitched. He did things while under those spells (Bukhari
IV:400, 490; VII:660; and Muslim III:5428). Under satanic
influence, he even put lies into the Qur'an! Once it is
admitted that he put lies into the Qur'an and did things
while under satanic influence, it opens the possibility that
the entire Qur'an could be satanic in origin.

Later Muslim authorities even went so far as to say
that he was at one time inspired by Satan to put some
verses into the Qur'an. They were later removed because
they were Satanic verses (Surah 53:19,20).

4. The Hadith tells us that "Allah made the prophet
    wealthy through conquests" (Bukhari III:495). Was
    he in it for the money? Some Muslims are ignorant
    of this Hadith and claim that Muhammad was poor
    like Jesus.

5. He did not keep the rules he imposed upon others.
    He had more than four wives (Bukhari I:268) and
    did not write a will (Bukhari IV:3, 4).

6. He commanded that anyone who fell away from
    Islam should be murdered (Bukhari IV:260; V:630).
    Volume IX is filled with death threats against
    apostasy (pages 10, 11, 25, 34, 45, 50, 57, 341,

342). These Hadiths contradict other Hadiths that say that no one ever leaves Islam (Bukhari I:6, 48).

The punishment of apostates reveals that Islam cannot uphold the freedom of religion, the freedom of speech, the freedom of assembly or the freedom of the press. The fact that Muhammad commanded that no churches or synagogues be allowed in Arabia is a telling argument that he was not a man of peace.

7.   The Hadith reveals that Muhammad had to ask forgiveness for sin more than seventy times a day (Bukhari I:71, 78; V:724). Since Muslims believe that prophets must be sinless, this means that Muhammad was not a prophet. Most Muslims claim that Muhammad was sinless despite the overwhelming evidence to the contrary.

8.   He was guilty of false prophecies:

The 100-Year Prophecy (Bukhari I:539). Muhammad predicted that no one would be left on earth after one hundred years.

The end of the world predictions (Bukhari IV:401). He gave signs for the end of the world.

9.   He kissed and caressed the idol of black stone set into the wall of the Kabah (Muslim II:2912, 2916). We cannot imagine Abraham or Jesus kissing a pagan idol and then commanding their followers to do so.

The Teachings Of Muhammad

Just as the Hadith gives us good reasons to question the integrity of Muhammad, his teachings recorded in the

Hadith give us even more reason to doubt he was a prophet.
The following is a brief list of some of the strange and
absurd teachings of Muhammad:

1. Adam was 60 cubits tall! (Bukhari IV:543).
   Then how tall was Eve? If they were that tall,
   how did we get here? Is it medically possible
   for him to be that tall? No. A three story high
   Adam would not have had a heart large enough
   to pump blood to his head.

2. Muhammad was a dog hater. He thought that
   angels could not enter a house if a dog was
   there and that black dogs were devils. Thus, he
   ordered dogs to be killed and forbade the
   selling of dogs (Bukhari IV:539, 540; and
   Muslim I:551, 552; II:3803, 3829).

3. Satan lives in the nose overnight. He can be
   flushed out if you snort water up and then out
   the nose (Bukhari IV:516; and Muslim I:462).
   How big is Satan? Is he in everyone's nose? Is
   he omnipresent?

4. Muhammad forbade the game of chess
   (Muslim IV:5612)! This makes no sense to me.

5. People turn into rats, pigs and monkeys
   (Bukhari IV:524, 627; and Muslim IV:7135).
   Abraham's father was turned into an animal
   (Bukhari IV:569).

6. Muslims have one intestine while non-Muslims
   have seven (Bukhari III:5113-5115)!

7. If you lift your eyes toward heaven while
   praying, your eyes will be snatched out
   (Bukhari III:862-863)!

8. One wing of a fly has poison but the other wing
    has the antidote to it (Bukhari IV:537).

9. We should drink camel urine as a medicine
    (Bukhari I:234).

10. Fevers are from the fire of hell and can be
    cooled by water (Bukhari IV:483, 486).

The Text of the Qur'an

Who wrote out the Qur'an? On what materials? Who
put the Qur'an together? Where did he find the materials to
do this? Why did he do this? Were others putting together
their own Qur'ans? Did these Qur'ans contradict each
other? How did one text gain dominance over all the
others? What happened to the other Qur'ans? Only the
Hadith gives us answers to these questions.

1. From Bukhari VI:509, we learn the following
    things:

    Muhammad did not collect the fragments of the
    Qur'an and make them into a manuscript.

    Some of the Companions of Muhammad were
    killed in battle and whatever surahs they had
    memorized died with them.

    Abu Bakr asked Zaid to collect the fragments
    of the Qur'an and arrange them into a
    manuscript.

    Zaid hesitated because the task was harder than
    sifting through an entire mountain.

2. The task was difficult because of:

The fragile nature of the fragments: palm leaves, stones, bones, etc.

The faulty memories of men (Bukhari VI:527).

The false claims of men (Bukhari VI:523).

Conflicting versions of the Qur'an (VI:510, 514, 523).

Contradictory orders of the surahs (VI:515, 518).

Allah caused verses to be abrogated or forgotten (Bukhari IV:57, 62, 69, 299, 393; VI:510, 511, 527).

Muhammad himself forgot and missed various parts of the Qur'an (Bukhari VI:558, 562).

3. Even after the manuscript was put together, they found that they had missed some verses (Bukhari IV:62; VI:510).

4. They tried to burn all the other Qur'anic fragments and manuscripts (Bukhari VI:510).

5. Uthman is usually credited for making the present text (Bukhari I:63; IV:709; VI:507, 510).

It is clear that the text of the Qur'an was not perfect and that conflicts arose which made it necessary to make one uniform text. That Uthman tried to burn all the other Qur'ans is clear. Yet, there are thousands of variant readings and there remain controversies about verses such as the one about stoning that were omitted by mistake.

The Contradictions and Variant Readings in the Hadith

One problem all Muslims face is that there are contradictions in the Hadith, conflicting readings and abrogations of Hadiths (Bukhari I:42, 47, 74, 78, 80, 81, 86, 102, 107, 112, 159, 160, 161, 179, 180; III:159, 161; and Muslim I:682, 685, 689, 699; II:2547, 2548). The footnote on Bukhari III:159 says,

> "Hadith number 159 contradicts the Hadith of Al-Hassan."

Evidently Allah was not capable of preserving a perfect text of the Hadith. On what grounds then can we assume that the Qur'an was kept perfect?

The Inspiration of the Qur'an

The mistakes in the Qur'an are well known. I list over one hundred such problems in the book *Islamic Invasion*. The following are a few of the more glaring problems that the average person has no problem seeing. All we need is ONE factual error to disprove the Qur'an. We are not talking about conflicts with theories but with brute facts.

1. Theological errors: The Qur'an is mistaken about what Christians and Jews believe (Surah 5:73, 75; 9:30).

2. Historical mistakes: The Samaritans (Surah 20:85, 97), Alexander the Great, etc.

3. Grammatical errors: Arabic scholars point out errors in Surahs 2:177, 192; 3:59; 4:162; 5:69; 7:160; 13:28, 20:66; 63:10, etc. The mistakes have to do with conflicts between gender and number.

4. Linguistic errors: Even though the Qur'an claims to be in pure Arabic (12:2; 13:37; 16:105; 41:44; 42:7), it has foreign words.

5. Scientific errors: Sun sets in a muddy pond (Surah 18:86), mountains never shake (Surah 16:15; 21:31; 31:10; 78:6,7; 88:19).

6. Moral errors: Muhammad justified the taking of his daughter-in-law away from his adopted son Ali so she could be in his harem (Surah 33:36, 38).

7. Mathematical errors: Did creation take place in six days (Surahs 7:51; 10:3) or eight days (Surah 41:9, 10, 12)? This is also an example of where the Qur'an contradicts itself. Many examples are given in *Islamic Invasion*.

8. Chronological errors: Puts Muslim vocabulary into mouth of Patriarch, prophets, etc. (Surah 2:128, 133 etc.). The words did not exist in Hebrew or Arabic at that time.

9. Biblical errors: The confusion of names, places, events and times, and they couldn't even get the name of Jesus right. He was the Son of God who died for our sins on the cross according to the Bible. The Qur'an contradicts this.

10. Political errors: Commands Jihad against apostates and non-Muslims (Surahs 4:91; 5:33; 9:5).

CONCLUSION

The Hadith and the Qur'an stand or fall together. It is clear that they are not from God and are false works.

PART 2: THE SECULAR APPROACH

Modern scholars such as Crook, Crone, Wansbrough, Rippin, etc., are giving us a totally different model of the origins of Islam and the Qur'an. Once you put aside the Qur'an and the Hadith, you begin to see that Islam created the Qur'an instead of the Qur'an creating Islam. Islam created a mythological Muhammad who is nothing like the historical Muhammad, if that was even his true name. The Qur'an had multiple authors from various locations who combined different legends and materials to make the stories found in it. It took 150-200 years for the Qur'an to appear. Muhammad never saw the present Qur'an and would disown it if shown it. He is not the source of it. This explains the contradictions and mistakes in it.

<u>Time Line</u>

7th Century	570	Muhammad's birth
	610	Muhammad's call to prophethood
	632	Muhammad's death
	650	Caliph Uthman
	691	First version of the mosque called "The Dome of the Rock.
8th Century	700	Legends & myths
9th Century	800	Traditions
		700,000 Hadiths
	850	Bukhari's Hadith
10th Century	923	Tabari's Commentary

1. No references to Muhammad as a prophet have been found in contemporary literature, rock inscriptions, or coins.

2. No manuscripts of the Qur'an exist before 150-200 years after Muhammad died. This allows a tremendous opportunity for myths and legends to arise.

3. The claim that Uthman compiled the Qur'an has no evidence to support it.

4. The claims that two "original" Uthman Qur'ans can be seen at Topkapi, Turkey, and in Tashkent, Russia, are false. The manuscripts are in the Kufic script that did not exist in the 7th Century. They are clearly from the 9th Century and are in 'landscape' format that was not used in the 7th century.

5. The present text of the Qur'an came from multiple authors using erroneous legends, myths, and stories. It has many additions, deletions, variant readings, and no primary source materials to support it. It is thus a corrupt text and cannot be trusted to tell us what Muhammad really taught or did.

6. The text and stories of the Hadith are as corrupt as the Qur'an. Where is the evidence to support its claims?

CONCLUSION

Muslims cannot demonstrate that the Qur'an is inspired. Instead, the evidence is 100% against it.

CHAPTER FOUR

WHAT IS THE MEANING OF JIHAD?

"It is our opinion that whoever claims the acceptability of any existing religion today-other than Islam-such as Judaism, Christianity and so forth, is a non-believer. He should be asked to repent. If he does not, he must be killed as an apostate because he is rejecting the Qur'an."

Shaikh Muhammad as-Saleh al-Uthaimin,
(*The Muslim's Belief*, p. 22.)

When seeking to understand what a particular organized religion teaches, it is important to distinguish between the *official teachings* of a religion and the *personal opinions* of someone who claims to follow that religion.

The Catholic View of Abortion

For example, what is the teaching of Roman Catholicism on the issue of abortion? The only way you can find out what it teaches on abortion is to examine general reference works and the official publications of the church to see what it has stated. Once you check out dictionaries, encyclopedias, theology books, etc., it is clear that abortion is condemned by the Catholic Church.

But what if you have a neighbor who is a Roman Catholic who believes in abortion? What if she says,

"Catholicism does not deny abortion. I ought to know because I am a Catholic and I believe in abortion."

The only rational response you can give to this person is that her *personal opinion* on the issue does not alter the *official teaching* of her religion. She may disagree with her church's doctrine but the fact that she does not believe in it does not alter what the Catholic Church teaches.

The Same for Jihad

The same distinction must be made when discussing whether the religion of Islam teaches Jihad. The only way to find out if it teaches Jihad and what that word means is to examine reference works and official statements made by its representatives.

What if you meet a Muslim who denies that Islam teaches Jihad or who gives a novel interpretation of it? His *personal opinion* has no logical or legal bearing on what the religion of Islam *officially* teaches concerning Jihad. *He may disagree with what Islam teaches but this cannot alter the fact that Islam teaches it.*

THE FIRST STEP

Let us take a trip to the local library to do some research on the subject of Jihad. The first step in doing research on any topic is to establish the meaning of the key word. Thus you must go to the *dictionaries* to see how they define the word "Jihad". You first consult general dictionaries and then religious dictionaries that have an entry on the subject. What will you find?

I. THE DICTIONARIES

Webster's Third New International Dictionary, p.1216:

A holy war waged on behalf of Islam as a religious duty; a bitter strife or crusade undertaken in the spirit of a holy war.

Webster's New Twentieth Century Dictionary, p. 985:

A Moslem holy war; campaign against unbelievers or enemies of Islam.

Webster's New International Dictionary, p. 1336:

A religious war against infidels or Muhammedan heretics.

The Random House Dictionary of the English Language, p. 1029:

A holy war undertaken as a sacred duty to Muslims.

Universal Dictionary of the English Language, p. 631:

"Contest, war" - A Mohammedan war against unbelievers, campaign against the enemies of Islam.

The American College Dictionary, p. 657:

A war of Muhammedans upon others, with a religious object.

Britannica World Language Dictionary, p. 686:

A religious war of Moslems against the enemies of their faith.

The Oxford Dictionary, vol. V, p. 583:

[struggle, contest, spec. one for the propagation of Islam.] A religious war of Mohammedans against unbelievers in Islam, inculcated as a duty by the Koran and traditions.

Collins Cobuild English Language Dictionary, p. 781:

A jihad is a holy war which Islam allows merely to fight against those who reject its teachings.

The American Heritage Dictionary of the English Language, p. 704.

A Moslem holy war against infidels.

Longman Dictionary of the English Language, p. 849:

A holy war waged on behalf of Islam as a religious duty.

The Harper Dictionary of Modern Thought, p. 327:

Jihad ("Holy War"). A fundamental tenet of traditional ISLAM obliging the believer to fight the unbeliever until the latter embraces either Islam or the protected status accorded only to those whose religions are based on written scriptures (i.e., Jews, Christians, Sabaeans), the "peoples of the Book". A Jihad must be officially proclaimed by a recognized spiritual leader.

II. THE ENCYCLOPEDIAS

Once you have consulted the dictionaries, the second step in research is to examine what the encyclopedias say on the subject. What will you find?

The New Encyclopedia Britannica, vol 6:

Jihad, also spelled jehad, Arabic jiohad ("fight" or "battle"), a religious duty imposed on Muslims to spread Islam by waging war; jihad has come to denote any conflict waged for principle or belief and is often translated to mean "holy war".

Islam distinguishes four ways by which the duty of jihad can be fulfilled: by the heart, the tongue, the hand, and the sword. The first consists in a spiritual purification of one's own heart by doing battle with the devil and overcoming his inducements to evil. The propagation of Islam through the tongue and hand is accomplished in large measure by supporting that which is right and correcting what is wrong. The fourth way to fulfill one's duty is to wage war physically against unbelievers and enemies of the Islamic faith. Those who professed belief in a divine revelation —Christians and Jews in particular—were given special consideration. They could either embrace Islam or at least submit themselves to Islamic rule and pay a poll and land tax. If both options were rejected, jihad was declared.

Collier's Encyclopedia, vol. 13, p. 587:

Jihad, from an Arabic verb meaning to struggle and persevere, denotes, in the history of Islamic civilization, religious war waged against heretics, unbelievers, and the enemies of the state or the community of Muslims. In early Islamic history "jihad" meant holy war, and, as a strictly Islamic phenomenon, it bears a strict relation to the spread of the faith by Muslims' arms. It was a duty to the Kharijits, a band of warlike rebels, and jihad was considered an obligation or command; and by them it was ranked as a sixth pillar of religion.

The Encyclopedia Americana International Edition,
vol 16, pgs. 91-92:

Jihad, an Arabic word meaning "struggle". As
a religious duty theoretically laid upon all
followers of Mohammed, jihad is based on the
concept that the Islamic faith, since it is of
universal validity, must be spread to all mankind,
by force of arms if necessary. In classical Islam,
jihad was to be directed against "people of the
Book" (that is, possessors of authoritative sacred
writings, above all Jews and Christians) until they
submitted to the political authority of Islam, and
against idolaters until they became Muslims. Sufi
mystics, however, often considered jihad as a
spiritual struggle against the evil within the self.

The Cambridge Encyclopedia, p. 637:

Jihad - the term used in Islam for "holy war".
According to the Koran, Muslims have a duty to
oppose those who reject Islam, by armed struggled
if necessary, and jihad has been invoked to justify
both the expansion and defense of Islam. Islamic
states pledged a jihad against Israel in the Mecca
declaration of 1981, though not necessarily by
military attack.

Academic American Encyclopedia, p. 418:

In Islam, the duty of each Muslim to spread
his religious beliefs is termed "jihad". Although
the word is widely understood to mean a "holy

war" against nonbelievers, jihad may also be fulfilled by a personal battle against evil inclinations, the righting of wrongs, and the supporting of what is good.

The Concise Encyclopedia of Islam, p, 209:

Jihad "Holy war", a Divine institution of warfare to extend Islam into the dar al-harb (the non-Islamic territories which are described as the "abode of struggle", or of disbelief) or to defend Islam from danger. Adult males must participate if the need arises, but not all of them, provided that "a sufficient number" (fard al-kifayah) take it up.

An important precondition of jihad is a reasonable prospect of success, failing which a jihad should not be undertaken. According to the Sunnah, a jihad is not lawful unless it involves the summoning of unbelievers to belief, and the jihad must end when order is restored; that is, when the unbelievers have accepted either Islam or a protected status within Islam, or when Islam is no longer under threat. It is impossible to undertake a jihad against Muslims.

III. HISTORICAL AND THEOLOGICAL WORKS

Now that you have consulted the dictionaries and the encyclopedias, you look in the card catalog to see if there are any specific textbooks that deal with the issue of Jihad. What do you find? There are many books written by Muslims and non-Muslims alike on the subject of Jihad.

The first work on the true meaning of Jihad comes from Sheik Abdullah bin Muhammad bin Hamid, the head cleric of the Sacred Mosque of Mecca, the holiest site in Islam. Mecca is to the Muslim world what the Vatican is to the Roman Catholic world. The pronouncements of the Meccan Mosque are tantamount to proclamations issued by the Pope. What does he say about the meaning of Jihad?

Praise be to Allah who had ordained "Al-Jihad" (Fighting for Allah's Cause)

(1) With the heart (intentions or feelings),

(2) With the hand (weapons)

(3) With the tongue (speeches, etc., in the cause of Allah) and has rewarded the one who performs it with the high rooms in the gardens of (paradise).

The Call To Jihad (Fighting For Allah's Cause) In The Holy Qur'an (Sahih Bukhari, vol 1, pgs. xxii-xl)

The Prophet Muhammad carried on inviting people to Allah and persisted in this invitation for 13 years.... And when Allah wanted to reveal His religion (Islam) and to fulfill His promise and to make victorious His prophet, Allah, the Most High, ordered him to emigrate to Al-Medina.... Then, at that time Allah permitted them the Jihad of fighting but he did not make it obligatory.... But after that He made "fighting" Jihad obligatory against all those who fight you.... Then Allah revealed in Sura Bara'at (Repentance, IX) the order to discard all the obligations (covenants, etc.) and commanded the Muslims to fight against all the pagans as well as against the people of the

scriptures (Jews and Christians) if they do not
embrace Islam.... So they were not permitted to
abandon "the fighting" against them (pagans, Jews
and Christians) and to reconcile with them.... At
first "the fighting" was forbidden, then it was
permitted and after that it was made obligatory....

So fight in the cause of Allah (for) Islamic
Faith (worshipping none but Allah alone) and
sincerely (for Allah's sake) and to make victorious
Allah's Religion till it becomes superior over all
religions.

To get ready for Jihad includes various kinds
of preparations and weapons (tanks, missiles,
artillery), airplanes (air force), naval ships (navy,
etc.) and the training of soldiers in these weapons
are all included under the meaning of the word
"force".

And now they (Muslims) have deserted the
Jihad and asked help from their enemies (i.e., non-
Muslims) and protection from the disbelievers
begging them, turning towards them, expecting
good from them.

Lest the reader think that Sheik Hamid is alone in his
understanding of the meaning of Jihad, let us look at other
statements.

"Jihad means the conquest of non-Muslim
territory. The domination of Koranic law from one

end of the earth to the other is...the final goal...of
this war of conquest."

Ayatollah Khomeini

"Jihad is a religious obligation. It forms part
of the duties that the (Muslim) believer must
fulfill; it is Islam's *normal* path to expansion."

Jacques Ellal

"The most important function of the doctrine
of Jihad is that it mobilizes and motivates Muslims
to take part in wars against unbelievers, as it is
considered to be the fulfillment of a religious duty.
This motivation is strongly fed by the idea that
those who are killed on the battlefield, called
martyrs (shahid, plur. shuhadda), will go directly
to Paradise. At the occasion of wars fought against
unbelievers, religious texts would circulate,
replete with Koranic verses and hadiths extolling
the merits of fighting a jihad and vividly
describing the reward waiting in the hereafter for
those slain during the fighting.

Jihad In Classical and Modern Islam, by
Rudolph Peters, p. 5.

"The sword is the key to heaven and hell,"
Muhammad told his followers. Six hundred years
earlier, Christ had said, "He who lives by the
sword shall perish by the sword." Muslims who
kill are following the commands of Muhammad,
but Christians who kill...are ignoring the words of
Christ. Therein lies perhaps one of the basic

philosophic differences, between Islam and
Christianity.

Jihad, by Robert Fregosi, pg. 22.

The Jihad originates in the Koranic teaching and was
practiced by Muhammad in his lifetime against Jewish and
pagan tribes in the Arabian peninsula, and soon after his
death against the Persians and against the Christian peoples
of the Byzantine empire, Syria and Palestine. Hundreds of
years later, it terrified Europe. "From the fury of the
Mahomedan, spare us, O Lord!" was a prayer heard for
centuries in all the churches of central and southern Europe.

The great expansion of Islam in the short time after its
inception was largely due to the militant spirit of the new
faith. A great many verses of the Qur'an enjoin on
Moslems to take up arms against polytheists, unbelievers
and hypocrites. The words used in expressing this
commandment are "Qital" (slaying, warfare) and "Jihad"
(going forth to fight in the holy war). This latter word is
more typical as its original meaning is striving with might
and main; and, as will be seen, the dedication of maximum
effort to the holy undertaking characterizes the
commandment. Although the wording of one verse (II.186)
implies that fighting is justified when the enemy has
attacked first, this is by no means the general rule. Nor is
there any substance in the argument which is sometimes
advanced to the effect that Jihad should be understood
primarily in the sense of moral endeavor and self-discipline
in the cause of service to Islam, and only secondarily in that
of holy war. The verses quoted below will show that the
emphasis is distinctly on warring against non-believers
with the object of propagating Islam, this being, by the

express injunction of the Qur'an, one of the primary duties of Moslems.

"O Prophet, make war on the unbelievers and hypocrites and deal rigorously with them; their home shall be Hell..." (IX.73).

"O believers, fight the infidels who dwell around you, and deal rigorously with them" (IX.124).

"Do not yield to unbelievers, but strive against them in a strenuous Jihad" (XXV.54).

"Fight for the cause of Allah with the devotion due to Him" (XXII.77).

"Fight valiantly for His cause so that you may triumph" (V.39).

"Whether unarmed or well-equipped, march on and fight for the cause of Allah with your wealth and your persons" (IX.41).

"Fight in God's cause; you are accountable for none but yourself. Rouse the faithful" (IV.86).

"Fight against the idolaters until idolatry is no more and Allah's religion reigns supreme" (II.189 and VIII.40).

"Fighting is obligatory for you, and you dislike it. But you may dislike a thing although it is good for you, and love a thing although it is bad for you" (II.212).

"Allah loves those who fight for His cause in ranks as firm as a mighty edifice" (I.XI.4).

"The true believers are those...who fight for His cause with their wealth and their persons" (XLIX.15).

"O Apostle, rouse the believers to the fight. If there are twenty amongst you, patient and persevering, they will vanquish two hundred; if a hundred, they will vanquish a thousand of the unbelievers" (VIII.67).

"When you meet the unbelievers, smite at their necks; at length when you have thoroughly subdued them, bind a bond firmly (on them), thereafter is the time either for generosity or for ransom until the war lays down its burdens" (XLVII.4).

In a number of verses the command to fight is supported by promise of rewards.

"Who is he that will loan to God a beautiful loan which God will double to their credit and multiply many times?" (II.245-246).

"Allah has given those that fight with their goods and their persons a higher rank than those who stay at home. He has promised all a good reward, but far richer is the recompense of those who fight for Him; rank of His own bestowal, forgiveness and mercy" (IV. 97).

"Those who believe, suffer exile and strive with might and main in God's cause with their goods and their persons have the highest rank in the sight of God" (IX.20).

"Those who...fought in the path of God have the hope of the mercy of God..." (II.215).

Those who fall on the battlefield in the course of holy war become martyrs.

"Those that...fought and died for My cause shall be forgiven their sins and admitted to gardens watered by running streams..." (III.194).

"Think not of those who are slain in God's way as dead; they are alive and well provided for by their Lord" (III.163 and II.149).

"As for those who are slain in the cause of Allah, He will not allow their works to perish.... He will admit them to the Paradise He has made known to them" (XLVII.5).

Other verses show God's displeasure with those who shirk their duty of fighting:

"And how should you not fight in the cause of Allah and for the helpless...?" (IV.77).

"Those who were left behind [in the Tobouk expedition] rejoiced in their inaction behind the back of the Apostle of God; they hated to strive and fight with their goods and their persons in the cause of God. They said, 'Do not go forth in the

heat;' say, 'The fire of Hell is fiercer in heat'"
(IX.81).

The above quotations are by no means exhaustive.
Clearly the Qur'an makes it the inescapable duty of every
Moslem to take part in fighting for the cause of God; only
the blind, the lame and the sick are exempt (XLVIII.17).
Whoever disobeys this commandment or tries to
compromise with the enemy is a "hypocrite" and must be
treated as an infidel. On the other hand, whoever takes part
in the fighting is not only promised the rewards of the
Hereafter, but in addition receives here below a share of the
booty taken.

> Except for a few verses which are revealed
> with reference to particular events such as the
> battles of Badr and Uhud, all the texts concerning
> Qital and Jihad have a general import. The
> obligation to engage in holy warfare is meant to
> persist, in the words of the Qur'an cited above,
> until God's religion reigns supreme. Therefore, if
> by God's religion is meant Islam in the specific
> sense, and if it is maintained that the
> commandments of the Qur'an go beyond the
> special circumstances and needs of the time of
> revelation, then it follows that the prescriptions
> concerning holy war place the Islamic community
> in a situation of potential hostility towards the
> non-Moslem world.

> *A Guide To The Contents Of The*
> *Qur'an* by Faruq Sherif, pgs 166-168.

"Exert your utmost" does not fully convey the meaning of *Jahidu*. It implies that the Believers should struggle against all the forces that stand in the way of Allah, as if to say, "You can please Allah and win His favor only if you exert your utmost in the way of Allah: struggle hard against all the persons, parties and forces which stand in Allah's way, which hinder you from Allah's way to turn you away from it, which do not let you follow Allah's way as His servants and force you to become their servants or servants of others. Such exertion and struggle will lead you to true success and become the means of obtaining the nearness of Allah."

Thus it must have become clear that this verse exhorts the Believer to fight his enemies on all fronts. On one side, he confronts Satan and a host of his followers, and on the second, his own self and its alluring temptations. On the third side, he has to fight many people who have swerved from the way of God, and with whom he is bound by close social, cultural and economic relations. On the fourth side, he is required to oppose all those religious, cultural and political systems that are founded on rebellion against God and force people to submit to falsehood instead of the Truth. Though these enemies employ different weapons, they all have one and the same object in view, that is, to subdue their victims and bring them under their own subjection. It is obvious that true success can only be achieved if one becomes wholly and solely a servant of God and obeys Him openly and also secretly, to the exclusion of

obedience to all others. Thus there is bound to be
a conflict with all the four enemies. Therefore the
Believer cannot achieve his object unless he
engages himself with all these hostile and
opposing forces at one and the same time and at
all events, and removing all these hindrances,
marches onwards on the way of Allah.

> *The Meaning of the Qur'an*, by S.
> Abul A"La Maududi, vol. III, pgs.
> 40-41

The Arabic words *Jihad-i-Kabir* imply three
meanings:

1. To exert one's utmost for the cause of
    Islam,

2. To dedicate all one's resources to this
    cause, and

3. To fight against the enemies of Islam
    on all possible fronts with all one's
    resources in order to raise high the
    "Word of Allah". This will include
    Jihad with one's tongue, pen, wealth,
    life and every other available weapon.

> *The Meaning of the Qur'an* by S.
> Abul a"La Maududi, vol. VIII, p. 98.

...the normal Arab practice of the razzia was
taken over by the Islamic community. In being
taken over, however, it was transformed. It
became an activity of believers against
unbelievers, and therefore took place within a
religious context. The Emigrants were described

as "striving with goods and person in the way of God." They were promoting one of the purposes of the Islamic community in trying to establish a region in which God was truly worshipped.

This transformation of the nomadic razzia has wider implications than are apparent from the English translations used. The word translated "strive" is *jahada*, and the corresponding verbal noun is *jihad* or "striving" which came in the course of time to have the technical meaning of "holy war". The change from the razzia to the *jihad* may seem to be no more than a change of name, the giving of an aura of religion to what was essentially the same activity. Yet this is not so. There was a change in the activity which came to be of the utmost importance as time went on. A razzia was the action of a tribe against another tribe. Even if two tribes were very friendly, their friendship might collide, and in a few years a razzia might be possible. *Jihad*, however, was the action of a religious community against non-members of the community, and the community was expanding. If members of the pagan tribes raided by the Muslims professed Islam, they at once became exempt from further Muslim raids. Consequently, as the Islamic community grew, the raiding propensities of the Muslims had to be directed even further outwards. It was this "religious" character of the *jihad* which channeled the energies of the Arabs in such a way that in less than a century they had created an empire which stretched from the Atlantic and the Pyrenees in the West to the Oxus and the Punjab in the East. It

seems certain that without the conception of the
jihad that expansion would not have happened.

Muhammad by W. Montgomery Watt, pgs 108-
109 (Oxford University Press).

The seventeenth book is the "Book of
Religious Wars and Expeditions" (Kiotab al-Jihad
Wa'l-Siyar). Jihad is a divinely ordained
institution in Islam. By many authorities, it is
counted as one of the pillars of Islam.
Theologically, it is an intolerant idea: a tribal god,
Allah, trying to be universal through conquest.
Historically, it was an imperialist urge masked in
religious phraseology.

Understanding Islam through Hadis by Ram
Swarup, p. 99.

To everyone acquainted with Islamic law it is
no secret that according to Islam the punishment
for a Muslim who turns to *kufr* (infidelity,
blasphemy) is execution. Doubt about this matter
first arose among Muslims during the final portion
of the nineteenth century as a result of speculation.
Otherwise, for the full twelve centuries prior to
that time the total Muslim community remained
unanimous about it. The whole of our religious
literature clearly testifies that ambiguity about the
matter of the apostate's execution never existed
among Muslims. The expositions of the Prophet,
the Rightly-Guided Caliphs (*Khulafa'-i
Rashidun)*, the great Companions (*Sahaba*) of the
Prophet, their Followers (*Tabi'un*), the leaders

among the *mujtahids* and, following them, the
doctors of the *shari'ah* of every century are
available on record. Al these collectively will
assure you that from the time of the Prophet to the
present day one injunction only has been
continuously and uninterruptedly operative and
that no room whatever remains to suggest that
perhaps the punishment of the apostate is not
execution.

*The Punishment Of The Apostate According To
Islamic Law* by Abul Ala Mawdudi, pgs. 17-19

A. The Proof from the Qur'an for the Commandment to Execute the Apostate

Here I wish briefly to offer proof that will quiet the
doubt in the hearts of those who, for lack of sources of
information, may think that perhaps the punishment of
death did not exist in Islam but was added at a later time by
the *mawlawis* (religious leaders) on their own.

God Most High declares in the Qur'an:

But if they repent and establish worship and
pay the poor-due, then are they your brethren in
religion. We detail our revelations for a people
who have knowledge. And if they break their
pledges after their treaty (hath been made with
you) and assail your religion, then fight the heads
of disbelief—Lo! They have no binding oaths in
order that they may desist (9:11,12).

B. Proof from the Hadith (Canonical Tradition) for the Commandment to Execute the Apostate

After the Qur'an we turn to the Hadith. This is the command of the Prophet:

1. "Any person (i.e., Muslim) who has changed his religion, kill him."

This tradition has been narrated by Abu Bakr, Uthman, Ali, Muadh ibn Jabal, Abu Musa Ashari, Abdullah ibn Abbas, Khalid ibn Walid and a number of other Companions, and is found in all the authentic Hadith collections.

2. Abdullah ibn Masud reports:

The Messenger of God stated: "In no way is it permitted to shed the blood of a Muslim who testifies that "there is no god except God" and "I am the Apostle of God" except for three crimes:

- he has killed someone and his act merits retaliation;

- he is married and commits adultery;

- he abandons his religion and is separated from the community.

Jihad, to struggle for a holy cause. According to Muslim belief, all healthy men, and occasionally women, must bear arms in the event of a holy cause that may or may not lead to war. Death in *jihad* is martyrdom. A warrior who gives his or her life for a holy cause will secure a beautiful place in paradise with special heavenly privileges. This is a good reason for foreign

powers not to provoke the Muslims to wrath.
Islam owes much of its popularity as a major
world religion to this tenet.

Understanding the Arab World by Louis Bahjat
Hamada, p. 164

IV. RECENT EXAMPLES OF JIHAD

Your next step is to go up to the librarian and ask if she
knows of any examples of Jihad in modern times. She will
point out that all the wars against Israel were Jihads. All the
recent terrorist acts from blowing up airplanes, the first
bombing of the World Trade Center in 1994 and its final
destruction on 9/11, the suicide bombings in Jerusalem, the
killing of American soldiers in Arabia and Germany, etc.,
were done in the name of Jihad.

She sends you to the computer to check out the
newspapers and magazines that used the word "Jihad" in
their report of recent terrorist activities. The computer
comes up with thousands of references in newspapers and
magazines where Muslims, in the name of Jihad, have
caused death and carnage around the world.

But then she hits on a rather recent example that is
crystal clear in revealing the violent nature of Islam: the
Salman Rushdie affair! He is the author of a book entitled,
The Satanic Verses. He was sentenced to death in the name
of Jihad. Several of the translators of his book were hunted
down and butchered in cold blood by Muslim fanatics. A
two-million dollar price was put on Rushdie's head by the
leader of Iran. He was thus forced into hiding for years. His
book is burned and banned in Muslim countries. Even the
Muslims in the West called for his death and the banning of

his book. If there was ever an example of the violent meaning of Jihad in modern times, this is it.

The reason the Jihad against Rushdie should be revisited is that the very same Muslim clerics who *now* claim, "Islam is a religion of peace," were calling for the murder of Rushdie! The very same liberal TV newsmen and newswomen who are now saying, "Islam is a religion of peace," said the opposite during the Rushdie affair. The word "hypocrisy" comes to mind.

Once you type the name "Rushdie" into the computer, thousands of references come up. It was a hot topic and all the newspapers and magazines wrote on the Jihad against him. After looking at some of the articles, you find several books were also written on the issue. What do you find?

"The Prophet did not urge his followers to love their enemies or to turn the other cheek. The Prophet of Islam preached his message during a bloody and violent period in Arabian history. He waged holy war—*jihad*—upon his enemies, the polytheists of Mecca, before overcoming them with superior numbers and force. On occasion, he behaved with utter ruthlessness towards his ideological opponents, like his former Jewish allies, the Banu Qurayza, whose males were massacred after the Battle of the Ditch (627 CE). The men—about 600 of them—were all beheaded, apart from those who converted to Islam; the women and children were sold into slavery" (p. 48).

"According to Ibn Taymiyya, anyone defaming the Prophet *must* be executed, whether he is a Muslim or not. There is disagreement among the experts about whether the blasphemer should be allowed to repent. Ibn Taymiyya comes down on the side of those who insist that even if the culprit repents, or converts to Islam in the case of a non-Muslim, he must be killed. Some authorities argued that Jews or Christians who cursed the Prophet should be killed unless they converted to Islam, and there are documented cases where this was applied" (p. 51).

A SATANIC AFFAIR: Salman Rushdie and the Rage of Islam by Malise Ruthven.

"Islam's Gangster Tactics" by Anthony Burgess:

"Evidently, there is a political element in the attack on *The Satanic Verses* which has killed and injured good if obstreperous Muslims in Islamabad, though it may be dangerously blasphemous to suggest it. The Ayatollah Khomeini is probably within his self-elected rights in calling for the assassination of Salman Rushdie, or of anyone else for that matter, on his own holy ground. To order outraged sons of the Prophet to kill him and the directors of Penguin Books, on British soil is tantamount to a *jihad*. It is a declaration of war on citizens of a free country, and as such it is a political act. It has to be countered by an equally forthright, if less murderous, declaration of defiance.

"...I gain the impression that few of the protesting Muslims in Britain know directly what they are protesting against. Their Imams have told them that Mr. Rushdie has published a blasphemous book and must be punished. They respond with sheeplike docility and wolflike aggression. They forget what the Nazis did to books—or perhaps they do not: after all, some of their co-religionists approved of the Holocaust—and they shame a free country by denying free expression through the vindictive agency of bonfires.

"They have no right to call for the destruction of Mr. Rushdie's book. If they do not like secular society, they must fly to the arms of the Ayatollah or some other self-righteous guardian of strict Islamic morality."

Source: *Sacrilege versus Civility: Muslim Perspectives on The Satanic Verses Affair* by M.M. Ahsan and A.R. Kidwaip, P. 75.

"In Defense of Sacrilege: Muslims—Nazis of Britain?:

"If members of Britain's community of some two million Muslims do not want to read Salman Rushdie's novel, *The Satanic Verses*, all they have to do is abstain from buying it or taking it out of the local library. They should not seek to impose their feelings about its contents—or, more probably, what they have been told about them—on the rather larger non-Islamic part of the population. Their campaign to have the book banned on the grounds that it blasphemes Islam, led to a demonstration over the weekend in Bradford in which, following the example of the Inquisition and Hitler's National Socialists, a large crowd of Muslims burnt some copies of the book...."

Source: ©*The Independent*, 16th January 1989—
"Dangers of a Muslim Campaign" (p. 73).

"Not the Book but the Muslim Protest is Distasteful":

"If members of Britain's Moslem community wish to pay £12.95 for the privilege of burning a copy of Mr. Salman Rushdie's, *The Satanic Verses,* in the privacy of their own homes, that is a matter for them. Many Christians who have struggled with Mr. Rushdie's impenetrable novels will warm their hands at the fireside. But *the* state is a society which, as they knew when they entered it, grants total tolerance to all faiths so long as those faiths do not conflict with that very principle of tolerance.

"What applies in the United Kingdom applies equally to the United States. What a secular society thinks of the prophet Mohammed is its own affair, and reason, apart from law, does not permit aggressive interference of the kind that has brought shame and death to Islamabad.

"I would much prefer that Khomeini argued rationally with the infidel West in the manner of the great medieval Arabs. But, instead of arguing,

he declared a holy war against argument. His
insolence is an insult to Islam."

Source: ©The Independent, 16th February 1989—
"Islam's Gangster Tactics" (pgs. 73-77).

"Unite Against Islam!" by Norman Stone:

"...Islam is the religion, after all, of the
ferocious Ayatollahs, of suicide-bombings and
hostage-taking; of the Afghan sects, who, no
doubt, will soon be meting revenge on
collaborators with the Soviets. Salman Rushdie
has learned this, in a very hard way....

"...The Mahdi is the enemy of mankind, and
particularly of womankind, and we need all the
allies we can get. The world as a whole must
unite to make sure that fundamentalist Islam does
not get away with it...."

Source: ©The Daily Telegraph, 19th February 1989—
"We Need Russian Help Against Islam" (p. 77).

LIMITS OF TOLERANCE

"There are few more difficult tasks, even or
perhaps especially in a liberal democracy, than to
define the limits of tolerance. A year after the
Ayatollah Khomeini first pronounced sentence on
Mr. Salman Rushdie, the difficulties for the
author, his publishers, and our own society have
become no easier to reconcile. Yet to almost all of
us, Mr. Rushdie's right to publish his book was,

and remains, beyond dispute. It has been dismaying to behold British Moslems publicly echoing the murderous threats of the Iranians. Only a month or two ago, several hundred Moslems gathered in Walthamstow to vote that the death sentence against the author should "remain in place". One Dr. Kalim Siddiqui has been strongly and openly associated with the call for Mr. Rushdie's death.

"If Moslem fundamentalism, and its bloodier manifestations, gain any hold in this country, they will have to be suppressed, employing the full vigour of the laws which were introduced to protect minority communities from racial harassment.

"We may all wish that Mr. Rushdie had not written his book. But he has done so, and we should continue to defend his rights, as Mrs. Thatcher and her Government have done with such credit. British publishers should encourage Penguin to proceed with the paperback edition. To flinch from publication now would be a surrender to those forces of fanaticism with which we cannot compromise if we are to sustain the traditional values and license of our own society. It is those values to which British Moslems must subscribe, however unwillingly, if they are to play a full part in British life, as we all wish that they should."

Source: ©The Daily Telegraph, 6th February 1990—
"Limits of Tolerance", pgs. 78-79.

"An Islamicist's Nightmare!" by Daniel Easterman:

"...Islamic law is not democratic: it is a system rooted in a series of supposedly infallible and unchallengeable texts, established by an elite body of scholars long since dead, and today interpreted and implemented by a similar elite. Shi'ite law is, if anything, less democratic than its Sunni equivalent: mujtahids achieve their positions, not by election, but by scholastic achievement....

"What would happen, then, if the law did allow the Muslim case against *The Satanic Verses*...fundamentalist zeal could draw up an ever-expanding list of additional titles for the attention of the courts....

"Now, what does that mean? For one thing, it means that books by Muslim heretics could be cited as blasphemous and banned in Britain. Studies by Muslim scholars challenging received wisdom about the Qur'an, *hadith*, Prophet, or law would meet the same censorship here as they already do in Iran, Saudi Arabia, or Egypt. Books by Baha'is—a group universally hated throughout the Muslim world—could be taken off the shelves in London or Edinburgh. Academic works on Islam would be scrutinized and, where found wanting, removed from university reading lists of libraries or bookshops. Older European texts deemed unflattering to Islam or Muhammad— Dante, Gibbon, Carlyle, Voltaire—could appear in bowdlerized editions.

"Remember, this is not paranoia on my part: books like these are already banned in most Muslim countries on the grounds of blasphemy. Why on earth would anyone stop at *The Satanic Verses* if they had the power to regulate anything and everything written about Islam...?"

Source: *Index on Censorship*, 4/90, pp. 9-11—
"A Sense of Proportion" (p.79).

"Rushdie Shemozzle is an Attempt to Blackmail":

"Mary Kenny was last week surely mistaken for once. The Rushdie shemozzle is not just a matter of freedom of expression versus censorship. *Islam is trying to blackmail us, with its preposterous death sentence and hints that hostages might be freed and diplomatic relations be restored if we ceased to protect Mr. Rushdie from its hit-men or at least consigned his book to oblivion.*

"Why should Muslims expect their religion to be protected from attack? Christianity is frequently assailed, sometimes blasphemously, but we do not respond by threatening murder and burning books and bookshops. Indeed, we expect our religion to be spoken ill of, since Jesus himself warned us that it would be. The proper reaction, we know, is to pity the blasphemer and pray for his salvation."

Source: ©*The Sunday Telegraph*, 24th June 1990—
"Rushdie Shemozzle is Attempt to Blackmail" (Italics ours.) (p.80).

"The Rushdie Affair"—Editorial:

"Many outrageous comments have been made in the wake of Iran's call for the murder of British author Salman Rushdie, but for sheer bloody-mindedness it is hard to match the remarks of Iran's charge d'affaires in London. Ayatollah Ruhollah Khomeini's command to faithful Moslems to kill Mr. Rushdie 'does not imply any political gesture by Iran, nor does it imply any interference in internal affairs of your country,' Akhoond Zadeh Basti said last week. 'If the purely religious-based opinion of a religious head is going to be interpreted politically, it is very unfortunate.'

"At the risk of taking Mr. Basti too seriously, what could be more political than calling for the assassination of a foreign national? It is the attempted extra-territorial application of Iran's capital sanction against blasphemy, without the inconvenience of a fair trial. It is a calculated assault on international law.

"It took a few days for Western nations to get up to speed in their political response, but the members of the European Community have now agreed to recall their ambassadors and restrict the movements of Iranian diplomats on their soil. Britain will go further by withdrawing its embassy staff from Tehran. West German Foreign Minister Dietrich Genser said the EC's action was partly in solidarity with Britain, 'but it is also a signal to assure the preservation of civilization and human values, the preservation of freedom of speech and expression.'

"Canada has balked at such forceful remonstrance; External Affairs Minister Joe Clark fretted that Canada should not overreact over a single issue. But Canada, no less than other countries, is vulnerable to the sort of mini-jihad Ayatollah Khomeini has launched. It is a Briton today; it might be a Canadian tomorrow, and not necessarily an author.

"Meanwhile, the government came within centimeters of a nasty blunder last week. An Ottawa association complained to the Prime Minister's Office that the Rushdie book constituted hate literature; the PMO sent the letter to Revenue Canada, whose officials promptly said they would detain any further shipments at the border pending an examination of their contents. Oh, what solace that would have given the sworn enemies of Mr. Rushdie; fortunately, officials decided over the weekend that there was no question of the book being hate literature, and new shipments may enter at will.

"The reaction of booksellers themselves has been mixed. It was sad to see Coles Book Stores Ltd. turn pale in the face of the Ayatollah's wrath and remove Mr. Rushdie's book, *The Satanic Verses,* from its 198 Canadian stores. Capitulation doesn't deter threats and acts of violence; it encourages them by showing that menace pays.

"To its credit, W. H. Smith Canada Ltd. said
it saw no reason to banish Mr. Rushdie's book
from its shelves: 'While W.H. Smith appreciates
that this novel has caused offense to certain
religious groups, our company policy is to make
available to our customers books which they wish
to purchase and which contravene no Canadian
laws.' (The book, we might note, has circulated
freely in Canada since its publication last year.)

"It may well be that international outrage at
Iran's actions plays into the hands of hard-line
Iranians, and that this whole crusade is a product
of domestic Iranian politics; but no country that
believes in international law can afford to let Mr.
Rushdie and his allies stand alone in their ghastly
predicament. The spiritual head of a nation has
given religious adherents in other nations an
exhortation to murder; if such practices are not
bitterly challenged, who among us is safe? Even
those who found *The Satanic Verses* offensive
have a stake in finding the Ayatollah's incitement
to murder many times more so."

Source: *Globe eMail*, Toronto, 21 Feb. 1989, from:
The Rushdie File Edited by Lisa Appignanesi and Sara
Maitland (Syracuse University Press) (pgs. 145-147).

Salman Rushdie Sentenced to Death by William J.
Weatherby:

"Obviously I have a view of the world which
is not theirs. I insist on my right to express it as I
think fit."   Salman Rushdie (Foreword)

"Mrs. Thatcher replied there were no grounds in which the government would consider banning the book. 'It is an essential part of our democratic system,' she wrote, 'that people who act within the law should be able to express their opinions freely.' Sir Patrick Mayhew, the attorney-general, decided the book constituted no criminal offense. Dr. Pasha then demanded the Home Office should ban the book (p. 130).

"Increasingly frustrated in their efforts to get the book banned, British Muslims staged angry demonstrations in several towns in the industrial North, where large Muslim communities lived. More than 7,000 people gathered in Bolton to watch a copy of *The Satanic Verses* being publicly burned. In Bradford, where more than 50,000 Muslims lived, another copy went up in flames outside the local police headquarters.

"The media had tended to ignore the early Muslim protests, but the book burnings were front page news. They awakened memories of Nazi and fascist demonstrations in the thirties. *The Independent* wrote that the Muslims' campaign 'not just against the book but against Rushdie personally does them no credit.' They should not seek to impose their feelings about the book on the 'rather larger non-Islamic part of the population.' Was the Islamic faith not strong enough to withstand some controversial fictional analysis in a book of literary merit that was 'written as a moral parable?' (p. 131).

"Both Rushdie and Penguin continued to
receive threatening letters and phone calls.
Rushdie tried to ignore them and live as freely as
he had before the protests began. He accepted an
invitation to make the keynote speech on apartheid
and censorship at a book fair in South Africa. He
was packing his bags ready to go to London
Airport to take a London-Johannesburg night
flight when he learned his visit had been canceled.
Some militant Islam fundamentalist groups had
threatened a holy war against the *Weekly Mail*, the
organizer of the book fair, if blasphemer Rushdie
arrived. Several bomb threats against the paper
and Rushdie were received (p. 132).

"Voices threatening to kill Rushdie on his
answering machine at home had forced him to
change his phone number and keep his address a
secret as much as possible. He was particularly
affected by a demonstration in Bradford at which a
copy of *The Satanic Verses* was nailed to a post in
a central square of the city before being set on fire.
His book had been crucified. For Rushdie it was
the last straw.

"'One simply cannot remember the last time a
book was burned in the streets of England,'
Rushdie said. 'You would have to go back really
a long time. They didn't just burn it; they nailed it
to a post first. They crucified it. To me it evoked
Nazism. The Inquisition. It made something snap
inside me. It made me start fighting back'"
(p.137).

The Rushdie Affair: The Novel, the Ayatollah, and the West by D. Pipes:

"The Canadian government temporarily banned imports of *The Satanic Verses*; worse, the prime minister finessed the freedom-of-speech issue by relegating the decision to Revenue Canada, a tax agency. The Prohibited Importation's Branch scrutinized the book but found that it did not fall within the legal definition of hate literature. Bonn called the incident a 'strain on German-Iranian relations.' The Swiss Foreign Affairs Department called in the Iranian ambassador and expressed its 'regret' over the incitement to murder Rushdie. But it was the Japanese government that came out with the limpist formulation of all: 'Encouraging murder,' it intoned, 'is not something to be praised.' Indeed, alone among the non-communist industrial states, Japan made sure that the Rushdie affair in no way affected its diplomatic relations with Iran (p. 157).

"Fundamentalist Muslims resident in the West furthered the ayatollah's cause in a number of ways, both non-violent and violent (p. 180).

"Khomeini's supporters also took to the streets. Fifteen hundred fundamentalist Muslims, mostly of Pakistani origins, demonstrated at the Place de la Republique in Paris, screaming, 'A mort Rushdie' ('Death to Rushdie') into the cameras. In the Hague, 5,000 Muslims gathered in front of the Ministry of Justice, burned

imitation copies of *The Satanic Verses* along with
pictures of the author, and called for Rushdie's
death. Nearly 2,000 Muslims protested noisily in
Manchester on February 24 and 10,000 in New
York City the next day, protesting outside the
closed offices of Viking. Also on the 25th, 1,000
Muslims marched in Oslo; the next day, 2,000
marched in Copenhagen. The protests in
Scandinavia were the first of such size in a decade
or more. Back in England, 3,000 Muslims
protested the Rushdie book in Halifax on March 3.
On the 4th, demonstrations took place in Sheffield
and Derby, complete with book burnings and
chants for Rushdie's death. On the 6th, another
3,000 Muslims marched in Derby and burned
copies of *The Satanic Verses*. And so on (p. 181).

"Then there was the atmosphere of
intimidation. A wide assortment of targets were
anonymously threatened with violence, leading to
additional police guards being posted here and
there around the globe. Politicians requiring extra
security included: in Canada, the minister of
revenue and the foreign minister; in Britain, the
prime minister, foreign secretary and home
secretary; and in France, the president of the
National Assembly. Artists were publicly
threatened in France, Nigeria, and Egypt. The
British television interviewer Peter Sissons asked
an Iranian diplomat, 'Do you understand that we
don't regard it as civilized to kill people for their
opinions?' Muslim zealots found this an
'insulting' question and threatened Sisson's life,
so he too had a police guard attached. A public

reading from *The Satanic Verses* in Austria had to be canceled due to telephoned bomb threats—one of which was traced back to the Iranian embassy in Vienna. Followers of Khomeini also issued dozens of threats to publishing houses and bookstores throughout the West.

"Threats with names attached were even more effective than anonymous ones. These fostered an atmosphere of intimidation the likes of which the West had not witnessed for decades. In Britain, several Muslim leaders endorsed Khomeini's decision, and some even swore to carry out the death sentence. The Union of Islamic Students' Associations in Europe issued a statement offering its services to Khomeini. Others were yet more outspoken, uttering statements that left the rest of the population aghast. 'I think we should kill Salman Rushdie's whole family,' Faruq Mughal screamed as he emerged from a West London mosque. 'His body should be chopped into little pieces and sent to all Islamic countries as a warning to those who insult our religion.' A London property developer told reporters, 'If I see him, I will kill him straight away. Take my name and address. One day, I will kill him.' Iqbal Sacranic of the U.S. Action Committee on Islamic Affairs announced that '...death, perhaps, is a bit too easy for him...his mind must be tormented for the rest of his life unless he asks for forgiveness to Almighty Allah.' Back in Bradford, the secretary of the Mosque Council, Sayed Abdul Quddus, said that Rushdie 'deserves hanging.' Parvez Akhtar, a financial adviser in Bradford, told a reporter that 'if Salman Rushdie came here, he would be torn to pieces. He is a dead man.' Newspaper reports filled with such statements made it appear that Khomeini's edict enjoyed support among Muslims of Britain, regardless of age, sex, social status and religiosity.

"Most striking, several prominent European converts to Islam endorsed the death edict, much enhancing its respectability. These included the French intellectual, Vincent Mansour (ne Vincent Monteil), and the Swiss journalist, Ahmed Huber. Cat Stevens, the former rock singer who converted to Islam in 1977 and changed his name to Yusuf al-Islam, told Muslim students in Surrey, 'He must be killed. The Qur'an makes it clear—if someone defames the prophet, then he must die.' Islam reiterated this view on television two months later, saying that if Rushdie turned up on his doorstep asking for help, 'I'd try to phone the Ayatollah Khomeini and tell him exactly where this man is (pgs. 182-183).

"The activism of Muslims during the Rushdie incident raised a host of new questions for Europeans: would the Muslims in their midst remain in ghettos of their own making, integrate themselves into Western life, or try to impose their political power and way of life on the majority of the population? Also, would they accept living in a secular order, or would they try to change it into something more familiar to them? (p. 214).

"A rally of Muslims in Toronto heard one of their leaders declare: 'We want to impose Islamic law. We don't care about the other laws of the world' (p. 218).

"Peregrine Worsthorne, a prominent columnist, expressed the dismay that was widespread:

Islamic fundamentalism is rapidly growing into a much bigger threat of violence and intolerance than anything emanating from, say, the [extreme right] National Front; and a threat, moreover, infinitely more difficult to contain since it is virtually impossible to monitor, let alone stamp out, the bloodthirsty anti-Jewish and anti-Christian language being preached from the pulpits of many British mosques.... Britain has landed itself with a primitive religious problem that we had every reason to suppose had been solved in the Middle Ages (pgs. 226-227).

"Freedom of Speech: The other key issue concerns freedom of speech, both in the Muslim countries and in the West. For Muslims in the Middle East and elsewhere, Khomeini's attack on Rushdie served as reminder of just how seriously personal liberties are lacking, and especially that of freedom of speech. As Amir Taheri has explained, Khomeini forced a debate on the long-deferred question, 'Can a man speak his mind without risking death or imprisonment?' (p. 248).

"The whimsically named League for the Spread of Unpopular Views, a West German organization, saw Khomeini's edict as a direct challenge to a central feature of Western civilization. 'The Rushdie case is a deadly earnest probe to see what freedom of expression in the West is worth. Should Rushdie be killed, it would be the first burning of a heretic in Europe in two centuries. The West would then carry the full responsibility, for it would have failed to have protected with all available means Rushdie and with him freedom of expression!' (p. 250).

"The West has to make it clear that the fundamentalist Muslims will gain nothing through threats and intimidation" (p. 251).

Rushdie has spoken out since Sep. 11, 2001 to correct all those who claim that Islam is a peaceful religion.

Well, by this time you have exhausted all the reference works on Islam that the library has. You have a good grip on what Jihad means according to the dictionaries, the encyclopedias, Islamic scholars, popular press, historians, theological works, etc.

First, *Jihad is clearly a major doctrine of the religion of Islam.* It is sometimes called the "sixth pillar of Islam". Its founder, Muhammad, stated that Jihad was the second most important thing in Islam!

Allah's Apostle was asked, "What is the best deed?" He replied, "To believe in Allah and his Apostle." The questioner then asked, "What is the next (in goodness)?" He replied, "To participate in Jihad (religious fighting) in Allah's cause."

(Bukhari, vol. 1, no. 25).

Second, *Jihad is commanded in the Qur'an and in the Hadith.* There are so many references to this fact that this is beyond all doubt.

Third, *it is the moral duty of all Muslims to participate in Jihad.* Any Muslim who says otherwise is voicing his personal opinion and not the official teaching of the religion of Islam.

Fourth, *in its non-violent form, Jihad means to strive with all your might against such temptations as alcohol, and for the conversion of non-Muslims to Islam.* In non-violent Jihad, people are encouraged to convert to Islam or to return to Islam by gifts of money, the promise of a job or university education, sexual favors, intimidation, evangelistic outreaches to non-Muslims, the distribution of tracts, books, tapes and videos promoting Islam, the promise of protection from rape in prison, etc.

Fifth, *in its violent form, Jihad has been invoked to justify every act of terrorism imaginable.* Waging war on a nation such as Israel or the United States is Jihad—the blowing up of school buses filled with children, bombing public transportation such as buses, trains, and planes, the killing of clergymen of other faiths, the murder of authors who speak out against Islam, the kidnapping and rape of women, the enslavement of non-Muslims, the assassination of political and religious figures, bombing buildings such as apartment houses, gang rape, the looting of homes, businesses, cities and nations, the burning down of neighborhoods and cities, the use of chemical and biological warfare against civilian populations, putting people in jail for criticizing Islam, torturing them and mutilating their bodies, etc. (See Fregosi's book, *Jihad*, for a history of Muslim Jihads against the West.)

But what if you run across a Muslim who says that Islam is a religion of peace and that Islam does not teach and practice Jihad? They are either ignorant of what Islam teaches or they are trying to deceive you. Either way, they are "apostates" because they have rejected the Qur'an and the Hadith.

CONCLUSION

How different is the religion of Jesus Christ, the crucified Son of God. He told His disciples to put away their swords and to use only the moral persuasion found in the preaching of the Gospel. Jesus did not come to found an earthly kingdom that would be forced on others against their will. He asks us to place our faith and hope in Him because of the love He showed on the cross when He died for helpless sinners. While Muhammad was the "prince of war", Jesus is the "Prince of Peace". Without Him, there can be no peace between God and man.

CHAPTER FIVE

WE WERE WARNED

"If you attack us, if Allah wills it, we will start the Third World War and the whole world will be destroyed. Every Muslim will fight until the last Muslim is alive."

Waris Khan Afirdi (9/13/01)

When everyone is saying, "Peace and safety, sudden destruction comes upon them" (I Thess. 5:3). With the collapse of the Soviet Empire and the demise of the cold war, the threat of Communism vanished in a twinkling of an eye. The tearing down of the Berlin wall is one of the greatest moments in human history. Russia was so impoverished by the arms race that it will take a long time for its economy to recover completely.

Communism was a religion that was harsh and cruel. It murdered more people than any other ideology in the history of mankind. The atrocities committed in the name of Marx and Lenin can only be compared to Hitler and his Third Reich, which fine-tuned mass murder into an art form.

In the flush of victory, the West in general, and America in particular, proclaimed that peace had finally been established on earth. A new world order of peace, prosperity and unity was just around the corner. We could safely dismantle our military and disarm our missiles of mass destruction. The threat to world peace was over. We could relax our guard and rest in the confidence that a heinous World War III would not happen in our time.

Thus the world was lulled to sleep while an old enemy of truth, justice, peace and democracy was gathering its strength for an all out offensive against the civilian populations of the West. This old enemy has attacked the West before. Its armies repeatedly invaded Europe for *eight* centuries. Some of these Jihads even reached the Vatican in Rome, parts of France and besieged Vienna, Austria on several occasions.

Jihad warriors destroyed everything they touched and left only mangled corpses and burned cities behind them. Their bloodlust and genocidal campaigns far exceeded any atrocities committed by the Crusades. They killed or enslaved women and children without mercy and shame. Their great goal was the destruction of Christianity itself and the forced conversion of the entire world to Islam.

While the West was disarming, Islamic terrorist nations were arming. While we were dismantling our missiles and nuclear warheads, they were buying and building intercontinental ballistic missiles capable of showering nuclear death on any city in Europe or America.

We stood in some ways like those few brave Americans who just before W.W. II warned people of the Nazi threat to world peace. They took the rhetoric of Hitler at face value and saw the buildup for war and terrorism across the world. Their warnings were ignored. "Peace in our time" was Chamberlain's swan song and the world was lulled to sleep while the Third Reich armed itself for war.

We have been in much the same situation. The Muslim threat to the peace and security of America is as real as was the threat of Nazism and Communism. If God does not intervene, the day will come when a mushroom cloud will yet appear over a major American city signaling death and destruction unparalleled in U.S. history.

The apostle Paul warned us that if the trumpet is not blown loud and clear, people will not prepare for war (I Cor. 14:8). We are watchmen who have the responsibility to warn the city of an approaching army of death and destruction. Isaiah tells us that if we fail to warn people of the coming war with Islam, their blood will be on our hands (Isa. 33:1-6).

In order to convince people that the religion of Islam constitutes a clear and present danger to the peace of the world, we must first demonstrate that the *fundamentalist* followers of Islam have the will and the desire to destroy us and, second, that they now have the means to do so.

What do we mean by the word *"fundamentalist"* Muslims? In every religion there are those who are faithful to the founder of their religion, who believe and act according to what he taught. They are the "True" followers of their religion.

- A fundamentalist Jew will follow the Torah.

- A fundamentalist Hindu will follow the Vedas.

- A fundamentalist Christian will follow the New Testament.

- A fundamentalist Mormon will follow the Book of Mormon, the Pearl of Great Price, and Doctrine and Covenants.

- A fundamentalist Muslim will follow the Qur'an and the Hadith.

We acknowledge that in every religion there are those who no longer believe in what their founder taught. Due to cultural, financial or social reasons, they still want to continue to call themselves "Muslim", "Christian", "Jewish", etc. while denying the core beliefs of their religion.

In order to do this, they take a "liberal" approach to their religion and explain away those aspects of their religion that embarrass them. Thus "liberal" Muslims will ignore the historical and traditional teachings of their religion and substitute a secularized Western approach that spiritualizes texts and turns them into symbols devoid of historical merit.

The majority of the followers of any religion, including Islam, believe in the founder of their religion. Even though liberals are always a minority within their religion, they are given a larger voice in the media than warranted by their numbers. This is why the liberal media has trotted out liberal Muslim clergymen to deny that Islam commands violence against non-Muslims. The truth of the matter is that liberal Islam is not Islam at all. It is a sham and sheer hypocrisy from beginning to end.

I. THE FUNDAMENTALIST MUSLIMS HAVE THE DESIRE TO DESTROY US.

The Qur'an commands its followers to launch jihads, holy wars of conquest, to force conversions to Islam. Since we will cite multiple passages later on in this book, just a few citations here will convince the intelligent reader that there *are* passages in the Qur'an that *do* teach violence.

"Fight against them until there is no persecution and the religion is Allah's only" (Surah 2:193).

"Fight and slay the unbelievers wherever you find them, and seize them, beleaguer them, and lie in wait for them in every stratagem of war" (Surah 9:5).

"Fight those who do not believe in Allah" (Surah 9:29).

"O believers, fight against the unbelievers near you" (Surah 9:123).

Muhammad sent his followers to attack defenseless caravans even in times of truce and peace. He then dispatched his armies to conquer and loot small villages and large cities. Ultimately, entire nations fell to the sword of Islam. Populations were put to the sword and great cultural treasures were either looted or destroyed.

Whereas Jesus told his disciples to put away their swords, Muhammad commanded his followers make war in his name. According to the Hadith, the second most important thing in Islam, according to Muhammad, is Jihad or holy war.

The bloodlust of Islam is thus rooted in a perverted religious impulse to kill and mutilate in the name of Allah. This is what makes it so insidious and wicked. The killing of innocent men, women and children in the name of Islam becomes a thing of praise and a badge of honor. The more you kill, the more Allah is honored—the greater the destruction, the greater the glory of Islam. This is why fundamentalist Muslims on 9/11 celebrated in Palestine, Detroit, Dearborn, Jersey City, Patterson, etc.

Listen carefully to what some influential leaders of Islam have said:

"We are at war against infidels. Take this message with you—I ask all Islamic nations, all Muslims, all Islamic armies and all heads of Islamic states to join the holy war. There are many enemies to be killed or destroyed. Jihad must triumph. Muslims have no alternative...to an armed holy war against profane governments.... Holy war means the conquest of all non-Muslim territories.... It will...be the duty of every able bodied adult male to volunteer for this war of conquest, the final aim of which is to put Organic law in power from one end of the earth to the other."

Ayatollah Khomeini

"The U.S. is the devil on this planet."

World Islamic Popular Command.

"Death to America, the Great Satan."

Muslim mobs in Egypt, Iran, Iraq, etc.

"Muslims must kill the enemies of Allah, in every way and everywhere in order to liberate themselves from the grandchildren of the pigs and apes who are educated at the table of the Zionists, the Communists and the imperialists.... The United States is a den of evil and fornication.... I will show all Americans that they will not be happy if they do not follow Islam."

Sheik Omar Adel-Rahman

"Any doubt about the need to struggle against the U.S. means being enslaved by the Great Satan

and losing the honor and the life the Islamic
Revolution has brought to this country and the
whole Islamic Ummah."

Ali Akbar Mohtashemi

"It is a matter of time...In 10 years you will
have quite a number of countries united under the
banner of Islamic fundamentalism."

Hassan al-Turabi

"There is fury, fury everywhere...Islam is
escalating and cannot be resisted. I pray that Allah
may tear apart America just as the Soviet Union
was torn apart...."

Sheik al-Tamimi

"Islam will bring America to its knees."

Louis Farrakhan

"I wanted to topple one [tower] into the other
and kill thousands *to send a message to Americans
that they were at war.*"

Ramzi Yousef, the mastermind of the blowing up
of the World Trade Center

"We will declare war on all U.S. facilities in
Indonesia."

(9/23/01) Ja'far Umar Thalib

"The United States is the No. 1 terrorist state
in the world. We are not afraid of the United
States, and we will teach them a lesson if they
attack Afghanistan."

(9/24/01) Mullah Fazlur Rahman

"I call upon all Muslims in the entire world to fight in the cause of Allah against America."

(10/7/01) Bin Ladin

Would it be permissible, by the law of Islam, to use a nuclear bomb during the prosecution of a Jihad?

"All things come from Allah," one student said, "The atomic bomb comes from Allah, so it should be used."

I then asked: Who wants to see bin Laden armed with nuclear weapons? Every hand in the room shot up.

"The Making of A Terrorist" by Jeffery
Goldberg (Reader"s Digest, Jan. 2002, pg. 76.)

If you think that threats like this are just hot air, come with me to ground zero at the Word Trade Center in NYC that was blown up by the disciples of bin Ladin on Sep. 11, 2001. Come with me to Scotland to the crash site of an airplane blown out of the air by Muslim terrorists.

Visit the gravesites of American citizens killed by Muslim terrorists in this country. In Washington D.C., the Muslims entered a home and killed everyone they found in the house. They took a nine-day-old baby and drowned him in the sink. They shot his ten-year-old brother in the head, then murdered his 23-year-old sister, his 25-year-old brother, their mother and a neighbor.

What can we say about the slaughter of thousands of innocent Christians in Egypt, Sudan, Iran, Iraq, Pakistan, Saudi Arabia, Kuwait, Indonesia, Malaysia, East Timor and wherever Islam can produce a reign of terror? WW III has already begun and we aren't even aware of it.

II. THE MUSLIMS HAVE THE MEANS AS WELL AS THE WILL TO DESTROY US

Islamic fundamentalists plan on putting together an Islamic empire composed of Turkey, Iran, Iraq, Afghanistan, Kuwait, Saudi Arabia, Qutar, Oman, Yemen, Egypt, Sudan, Libya, Algeria, Morocco, Tunisia, Nigeria, and the former Muslim Soviet states such as Uzbekistan.

Their plan is on schedule and they are taking over country after country while the West sleeps securely with its naive dreams of endless peace and prosperity of a new world order called the Pax Americana.

Listen to politicians and other leaders trying to wake up America:

> "The trial and subsequent conviction of the terrorists that bombed the World Trade Center and planned other terrorist acts should put to rest any doubt about the deadly threat to American citizens posed by radical extremists."
>
> Henry Depippo, Federal Prosecutor of Sheik Adbel

> "Each day's headlines demonstrate the timeliness this important analysis of the emerging trans-national radical Islamic movement...and the growing danger that extremist Islamic elements may seek to exploit our present vulnerability to missile attack with devastating results."
>
> Frank Gaffney, former Assistant Secretary of Defense for International Security

> "The agenda of these people is to attack us for what we are...It's something very hard for

Americans who live in a multi-cultured and
secular society to understand."

L. Paul Bremer, former head of the counter
terrorism office for the State Department

"[Muslim fundamentalists] make no secret of
their contempt for democratic politics."

Bernard Lewis

"The public must always remain vigilant
against acts of terrorism to ensure that terrorism
does not become commonplace in this country as
it has in many other countries."

William Sessions, former Director of the FBI

"Today we have no protection from even a
single ballistic missile."

Ambassador Henry F. Cooper

"In short, the coming Islamic Empire will be a
world power in every sense of the word whose
people will share a vibrant religion and a common
Islamic culture. Like its Muslim predecessors, the
Islamic Empire of the early 21st century will also
have an appetite for territorial expansion and
military conquest. A modern, worldwide jihad
against non-Muslim populations and societies
complete with nuclear weapons promises to bring
the highest casuality rates in the history of
mankind. World War III, if it does come, will
probably occur between the Islamic Bloc and the
Western nations. It will be the deadliest war ever
fought by Humanity."

Anthony Dennis

"It doesn"t matter what they tell you - Islamic
fundamentalism is a worldwide menace....

Allah is rapidly equipping Khomeini's followers
with a sword to carry out their master's wishes. He
has offered Islam the fire in which the Koran says
those who follow false faiths are destined to burn:
nuclear weaponry. He has also provided the long
range missiles needed to use it. According to the
late Imam's logic, there may be only one just and
righteous thing to do: employ this technology to
wipe out recalcitrant heathens like you and me."

Howard Bloom

On Oct 5, 2001, the Los Angeles Times reported that
the True goal of Bin Ladin was the creation of a super-
Islamic empire that embraced the entire Middle East.

Al-Qaeda's goal, in Bin Ladin's words, is "to unite all
Muslims and establish a government which follows the rule
of the caliphs".… Al-Qaeda's goal, therefore, is to
overthrow nearly all Muslim governments, which Bin
Ladin views as "corrupt", to drive Western influence from
those countries and eventually to abolish state boundaries
(A18).

With the break up of the Soviet military complex,
fundamental Muslim nations have been able to buy intercontinental ballistic missiles which are capable of striking
anywhere on the planet. They have nuclear bombs that can
fit into a steamer trunk and it is feared that such a device
may already be in this country. There is a real danger that
we will one day face nuclear blackmail just as we faced oil
blackmail in the 1970's.

Netanyahu states this clearly in his interview with
Michael Savage on September 16, 2001:

"I think what's important is to understand that
what you saw in New York was a wake-up call
from hell.... If the Islamic militant terrorist groups
are not stopped, then the next thing you'll see...is
not going to be a car bomb...but a nuclear bomb."

The religion of radical Islam presents a clear and
present danger to the most basic human rights, civil rights
and women's rights. Whenever and wherever it gains
control, tyranny and oppression follow. Those who ignore
this sober judgment of history will pay the price by losing
their liberty and their life.

CHAPTER SIX

AN ISLAM IQ TEST

The following propositions will test your knowledge of Islam. Mark each answer by checking it as True or False.

1. The Qur'an refers to people, places, things, and events that are nowhere explained or defined within the Qur'an. True____ False____

2. These things were not explained because it was assumed that the people hearing the Qur'an already knew of them. True____ False____

3. Some passages in the Qur'an would be unintelligible without recourse to pre-Islamic history. True____ False____

4. All Islamic scholars use pre-Islamic history to explain parts of the Qur'an. True____ False____

5. Thus it is both legitimate and proper to use pre-Islamic history to explain the Qur'an. True____ False____

6. Yusif Ali does this when it comes to such things as the she-camel, the elephant army, the 12 springs, the youths in the cave, the blind man, and many other things found in the Qur'an. True____ False____

7. Mecca was a pre-Islamic pagan center of worship.
                           True_____   False_____

8. The Kabah in Mecca was a pagan temple filled with
    360 idols.   True_____   False_____

9. Archeologists have found three other ancient
    Kabahs in Arabia.   True_____   False_____

10. The pagans prayed by bowing down toward Mecca
    several times a day.   True_____   False_____

11. The pre-Islamic pagans made a pilgrimage to
    Mecca.   True_____   False_____

12. When the pre-Islamic pagan idolaters got to Mecca,
    they ran between two hills. True_____   False_____

13. They ran around the Kabah 7 times.
                           True_____   False_____

14. The pagans kissed the large black stone on the wall
    of the Kabah.   True_____   False_____

15. The idolaters sacrificed an animal.
                           True_____   False_____

16. The pagans threw a magical number of stones at a
    pillar of the Devil.   True_____   False_____

17. The pre-Islamic pagans held their public meetings
    on Friday instead of Saturday or Sunday.
                           True_____   False_____

18. The pagans fasted during the day and feasted at
    night for one month.   True_____ False_____

19. The pagan fast began and ended with the Moon in
    its crescent phase.   True_____ False_____

20. The pagans gave alms to the poor.
                                  True_____ False_____

21. The pagan idolaters performed ritual washings
    before prayers.   True_____ False_____

22. As one of their washings before prayer, the pagan
    idolaters snorted water up and then out of their
    nose.   True_____ False_____

23. The pagans cut off thieves' hands.
                                  True_____ False_____

24. The pagans forbade marrying sisters.
                                  True_____ False_____

25. They forbade the eating of swine flesh.
                                  True_____ False_____

26. In pre-Islamic Arabian genealogies, Ishmael is
    nowhere mentioned as the father of the Arabs.
                                  True_____ False_____

27. Abraham, the father of Ishmael, was not an Arab.
                                  True_____ False_____

28. Hagar, the mother of Ishmael, was an Egyptian and
    not an Arab.   True_____ False_____

29. Since his mother and his father were not Arabs, Ishmael was not an Arab.   True_____ False_____

30. Ishmael could not be the "father" of the Arabs because they already existed before he was born.
True_____ False_____

31. According to the historical evidence, Abraham and Ishmael lived in Palestine.   True_____ False_____

32. Abraham and Ishmael never lived in Mecca.
True_____ False_____

33. Abraham and Ishmael never built the Kabah.
True_____ False_____

34. Abraham and Ishmael never established the rituals connected with the Kabah such as the Pilgrimage.
True_____ False_____

35. According to Arab history, the Kabah at Mecca was built by Kosia, Muhammad's pagan great-grandfather.   True_____ False_____

36. The title "Al-Ilah" was used by pagan Arabs in reference to one of the gods worshipped at the Kabah.   True_____ False_____

37. The word "Al-Ilah" was shortened into "Allah".
True_____ False_____

38. The Moon-god was called "Al-Ilah" and then "Allah" by some Arab pagans in southern Arabia.
True_____ False_____

39. Al-Lat, Al-Uzza, and Manat were worshipped by the pagan Arabs as "the daughters of Allah".
                                        True_____   False_____

40. Muhammad's father lived and died as a pagan and yet the word "Allah" was part of his name.
                                        True_____   False_____

41. Yusuf Ali points out in his translation of the Qur'an that the Moon was worshipped as a god by pagan Arabs.   True_____   False_____

42. Many of the pagan rituals associated with the worship of Allah and his daughters were incorporated into the Qur'an and are now part of Islam.   True_____   False_____

43. The religion of Islam has adopted the name, the rituals and the crescent Moon symbol of the pagan Arab Moon-god.   True_____   False_____

44. Some of the material found in the Qur'an can be traced back to pre-Islamic pagan Arabian religions.
                                        True_____   False_____

45. The people of Muhammad's day are recorded in the Qur'an as saying that Muhammad took old wives' tales and myths and put them into the Qur'an.
                                        True_____   False_____

46. The Qur'an warns against asking questions about Islam because if the answers are revealed, you will lose your faith in Islam.   True_____   False_____

The key to the answers:

All the above propositions are true! If you got all 46 correct, you are a genius. But if you answered false on any of the propositions, you do not know the truth about Islam.

CHAPTER SEVEN

TOP QUESTIONS ABOUT ISLAM

Question #1—Is "Allah" just another name for God?

Answer: Yes and No. It all depends on what you mean by "Allah." If you view it as a generic term, this means it is an empty term denoting nothing except the bare concept of "deity." When a word can mean anything and everything, then it means nothing. The Hindu pantheist could use the word "Allah" to describe the entire universe. Louis Farrakhan uses it to describe himself. It can be applied to idols.

Fundamentalist Muslims are not happy with the generic view of the word "Allah" and do not want anyone to use it except in reference to the God of the Qur'an. Thus they have made it illegal in such places as Malaysia for other religions, such as Christianity, to use the word in reference to their God.

Perhaps the problem revolves around two deeper questions:

1. Do all religions worship the same God?

2. Do Muslims worship the same God as Christians?

Do all religions worship the same God just under different names? Are all religions "true" in the sense that they worship the same God? Since it is claimed that the

God of the Bible can be worshipped under any name, it would only be logical to examine the Scriptures to see if it does in fact teach this. But when we look into the Bible, we find that it does not teach that all religions worship the same God just under different names. That this is true is demonstrated by the following propositions:

1) The First Commandment says that we are not to worship any other God than the One who has revealed Himself in the Bible (Ex. 20:3-4).

2) If all religions worshipped the same God under different names, there would be no idolatry, no false prophets, and no false religions. Yet, the Bible condemns all three. For example, Jesus warned us about "false prophets" in Matt. 7:15. Yet, if all religions were true, there could be no "false" prophets.

3) Throughout biblical history, the worship of Baal, Molech or any of the other gods of the Fertile Crescent was not viewed as the worship of the God of Israel just under a different name. Any attempt to mix other gods with the God of Israel was condemned by the Prophets and the Apostles. For example, II Cor. 6:14-17 condemns any attempt to mingle Christ and Baal as if they were the same deity.

4) According to Rom. 1:18-25, all the gods of other religions were invented by those who rejected the light of natural revelation and created gods in their own image. Thus pagan religions are not the result of man's search for God but the result of his running from God! As

a matter of fact, no one is searching for the true God according to Rom. 3:10-18.

5) The God of the Bible revealed the names by which he wishes to be addressed and worshipped (YHWH, Elohim, Adonai, Theos, Kurios, etc.). The Jews were not allowed to make up their own names for God but were limited to revealed names.

6) Even though some people have speculated that the names of pagan gods such as Baal may have come from the same basic Semitic linguistic root as Elohim, this does not linguistically, logically or historically imply that the Jews ever thought that "Baal" was just another name for the God of Israel. While a linguistic root may imply a common language, this does not logically imply a common deity. The prophets never viewed Baal as the God of Israel because of a shared linguistic stem.

7) When the Jews and Christians translated the biblical names for God into other languages, they never used specific names for specific pagan deities. For example, the Septuagint did not use the Greek name Zeus or the Egyptian name Ra as a translation for the Hebrew YHWH, as that would confuse pagan gods with the true God.

8) Jews and Christians used generic terms for deity as a translation for the names of God found in the Hebrew and Greek Bible. Thus YHWH was translated as Theos and Kurios in the Septuagint and in the New Testament.

9) The use of a generic term for "deity" in a foreign language translation of the Bible does not logically or historically imply that the translators believed that the God of the Bible was synonymous with any god that was designated by the same generic terms. Thus the use of Theos as a translation of Elohim did not logically imply that the Jews believed that Zeus or some other Greek god was the God of the Bible.

10) The fact that Jews and Christians would translate the names of God into different languages long after the Bible was completed does not logically imply that pagan gods who shared the same generic terms were viewed as being the God of the Bible.

11) In logic, a formal similarity in name does not imply a substantial agreement in concept. For example, all major pagan religions such as Hinduism and cults such as Jehovah's Witnesses and Mormons use the English word "God" when referring to their deity. Yet, while they use the same English word for deity that Christians use, they do not worship the same God that Christians worship.

12) The God of the Bible is not a vague "thing" that can be defined any way you please. The true God has revealed prepositional facts about Himself in the Bible. For example, the God revealed in the Bible is a personal, infinite and Triune Being of Father, Son, and Holy Spirit. Any concept of "God" that is less than that is not true according to the Bible.

13) The Apostle John used the concept of the
Trinity as a way to test other concepts of God.
He tells us in I John 2:22 that:

"Such a man is an anti-Christ – he who denies
the Father and the Son."

John's words cannot be any plainer. Any religion that
denies the Father and the Son is an "anti-Christ" religion
and cannot in any way be confused with true biblical
religion. But what if someone claims that he worships the
Father while denying the Son? John answers this in I John
2:23;

"No one who denies the Son has the Father;
whoever acknowledges the Son has the Father
also."

The Bible is clear that any religion that does not teach
the doctrine of the Trinity is an anti-Christ religion.

Lastly, since all religions contradict each other on
essential concepts such as God, man, sin and salvation,
either one religion is true and all the others are false or they
are all false. But they cannot logically all be true.

Conclusion

No matter how you look at it, the idea that all religions
worship the same God just under different names is a very
ignorant and foolish belief. It contradicts logic, history and
the science of comparative religion. It is actually an insult
to the major religions of this world which have very
carefully defined their concept of deity so as to distinguish
their god from all other gods.

Question#2—But isn't "Allah" just the Arabic name for God?

Answer: Given the laws of logic, linguistics, history and exegesis, the answer is "No!" "Allah" is not just another name for the one true God. In reality, in its name and concept, Allah is as pagan as Baal or Zeus. That this is true can be seen from the following propositions.

THE FACTS OF HISTORY

Perhaps the best way to answer this question is to look at it from the viewpoint of how Islam has actually treated Christians throughout history.

First, Islam's treatment of Christians underwent a drastic change as Muhammad's ministry developed. In the early days, when Muhammad wanted the Christians to accept him as their "apostle," he claimed that the Arabian deity "Allah" was actually the God of the Bible. Thus, Muslims supposedly worshipped the same deity that Christians worship.

In the Meccan Surahs of the Qur'an, Muhammad praised the Christians and even called them the "people of the book". These early statements were made in the hope that the Christians would convert to Islam.

But the Christian and Jewish tribes in Arabia refused to acknowledge that "Allah" was their God. They knew that Allah was a pagan Arab deity and had nothing to do with the God of the Bible. Muhammad ordered that all Jews and Christians be driven out of Arabia and that no church or synagogue ever be allowed on Arabian soil. The armies of Islam have always slaughtered Christians and Jews whenever they conquered a nation. One can think of what the Muslims did in Armenia as an historical example of this.

AN INHERENT CONTRADICTION

There is thus an inherent contradiction in the teaching of Muhammad concerning Christians. When Islam first comes into an area where there are Christians, the Muslims will say, "We Muslims worship the same God you do. Allah is the God of the Bible." Now, if this were true, then Christianity would be as "true" as Islam and you would not expect that Muslims would persecute them. After all, they supposedly all worship the same deity. But instead of leaving Christians free to practice their religion, as soon as Islam is in control of a country and establishes Islamic law, it then changes its approach and seeks to destroy Christianity in one Jihad after another.

A PRESENT EXAMPLE

What has now happened in Malaysia is a good example of how Muslims change in their attitude toward Christians depending on who is running the government.

When Malaysia was under Colonial rule, the Muslims said that their god, "Allah", was the God of the Bible. They allowed Malaysian Christians to use the Arabic word "Allah" when worshipping the Christian God. But now that Islamic law has been imposed on the country, it is now illegal for Christians to use the word "Allah" in reference to the Christian God! The Islamic government of Malaysia is presently confiscating and destroying all Bibles, hymnals, books and tracts that use the word "Allah" to refer to the Christian God. Why? The Islamic government of Malaysia

has ruled by decree that since "Allah" is NOT the God of
the Christians but only the god of the Muslims, then
Christians cannot use "Allah" in reference to their God!

THE PROBLEM AS WE SEE IT

Any rational person can see that the Muslims are trying
to have it both ways. In the West, they tell Christians that
Muslims worship the same God Christians worship. But in
countries under Islamic law, the Christians are persecuted
as "infidels", their churches burned and their people
murdered because they are NOT worshipping the same
God! This is why Christians are now forbidden by Islamic
law to even use the word "Allah" as a name for the God of
the Bible. This is why Christians in Saudi Arabia are not
allowed to build any churches. This is why the Pakistani
Islamic government has passed Penal Codes 294 and 295
which mandate the death penalty for the "crime" of
insulting Muhammad or Islam.

THE NAME "ALLAH"

Having examined the history of Islam and its
persecution of Christians, we now turn our attention to the
Arabic word "Allah". Is it really a proper name for the God
that Christians worship?

The following propositions will reveal that the word
"Allah" should not be used as a name for the God of the
Bible.

1. It is not a BIBLICAL name for God. The Patriarchs,
Prophets, Jesus and the Apostles never at any time prayed
to or worshipped "Allah".

2. It is not a REVEALED name for God. God revealed to the prophets in the Bible many different names by which He wanted men to call Him. But not once in the Bible did He ever reveal that "Allah" was His name.

3. In pre-Islamic times, "Allah" was a pagan name for a pagan deity among pagan Arabians.

4. Christians and Jews did not use "Allah" because it referred to a specific pagan deity.

5. In Southern Arabia, "Allah" was the title of the moon god who was married to the sun goddess. Together they had three daughters who were called the "daughters of Allah".

6. Throughout Arabia, Allah was viewed as only one of the "high" gods who was worshipped at the Kabah in Mecca.

7. The "daughters of Allah" were worshipped by the tribe into which Muhammad was born.

8. The Qur'an does not explain who "Allah" was because Muhammad assumed that the pagan Arabians already knew who he was. He was right. Allah was one of the 360 pagan gods worshipped at the Kabah!

9. As "Allah" slowly became a generic name in the Middle East and in Asia for deity in general, other religions used it as an Arabic name for their gods. But this does not logically imply that they believed that the god of Islam was their god. The name may have been the same but the concept different.

10. By the 19th Century, because of the dominance of Islam in the Middle East, the word "Allah" was used as a generic name for deity in the Arabic Bible. This was done

by British missionaries, who used "Allah" as a means to appease their Muslim oppressors and to escape death. But the time has come to correct their error and to tell the truth that "Allah" is a pagan name for a pagan god.

11. Modern Islamic countries such as Malaysia have decreed that the name "Allah" is the exclusive name of the god of Islam and not the God of Christians. Thus the Malaysian government has decreed that Christians may NOT use "Allah" in their bibles, books or hymns. They are in the process of confiscating and destroying all non-Muslim literature which uses the word "Allah".

12. New translations have come out which do not use "Allah." Instead, the translators go back to the names for God in their native language BEFORE the Arab armies conquered their country.

Since the Muslims are now saying that the word "Allah" is NOT a generic term for deity in general but it is a name that refers specifically to their concept of deity, the intelligent Christian cannot use the word "Allah" for God.

THE CONCEPT OF ALLAH IN ISLAM

The use of the generic Arabic word "Allah" in a 19th century Arabic translation of the Bible does not have any logical bearing on the issue of whether or not the god of Islam and the God of the Bible are the same God. In logic, formal similarities mean nothing.

The real issue is whether the concept of "Allah" in Islam is the same as that of the Christian God. If they are defined differently and have different or contradictory attributes, then there is no logical way to escape the conclusion that they are different deities.

The fact is that the Triune God of the Bible is not Islam's Allah. Thus the god of Islam is not the God of the Bible any more than it would be proper to say that the "God" of the Jehovah's Witnesses is the Christian God.

The following propositions demonstrate to the rational mind that Allah is not the God of the Bible. For the complete documentation, please consult my book, *The Islamic Invasion* (Christian Scholars Press).

1. Since Islam denies that Jesus is the Son of God and that God is a Father, it "denies the Father and the Son" (I John 2:22-23). Thus Islam is an anti-Christ religion. It cannot be both a biblical religion and an anti-Christ religion at the same time.

2. Allah's attributes are radically different from the biblical God. For example, Allah is unknowable and unpredictable. He is not a Trinity. He did not become incarnate for man's salvation. He is not a person or a spirit. He is not limited by anything, not even by his own nature. It is impossible to enter into a personal relationship with Allah, etc.

3. Just because you believe in one god does not logically imply that you have the right one. A Greek pagan could have proclaimed Zeus the one true God just as Muhammad proclaimed Allah to be.

4. The irrefutable fact that Muslims have consistently persecuted Christians as "infidels" reveals that when "the rubber meets the road" Muslims believe that their god "Allah" is NOT the same God that Christians worship. Otherwise, Christians would have never been viewed or treated as infidels.

Conclusion

The Muslim god "Allah" is not the same God that Christians worship. The vast majority of Muslims know this to be true. This is why they call Christians "infidels" and persecute them. Thus, liberal Muslims in the West who claim otherwise, do so as an evangelistic tool to convert ignorant and unwary Westerners to Islam. That they knowingly and openly use deception is not right and it does not speak well of the religion of Islam.

***Question #3**—Are we guilty of racism and hate speech if we criticize Islam?*

Answer:

1. To be against Islam is not racism because Islam is not a race but a religion. There are more Asian Muslims than Arab Muslims in the world. In the U.S., African-Americans comprise over 50% of the Muslims. Thus Islam is not made up of "Arabs" per se. The majority of Arabs and Palestinians in the US are Christians, not Muslims. Thus, anyone who thinks that "Arabs" and "Muslims" are synonymous terms is a racist.

2. To criticize the religion of Islam is not "hate speech" because all religions, including Islam, criticize each other. Freedom of religion means the right to discuss what you believe about other religions as well as what you believe about your own religion.

The liberal media has joined forces with the federal government to promote ten liberal lies:

TEN LIBERAL LIES

1. It does not matter what you believe as long as you are sincere.

The Truth: The terrorists were sincere in their beliefs. Their sincere beliefs led them to murder thousands of people. Thus it does matter what you believe if it leads to the destruction of the property and lives of others.

2. It does not matter what you believe as long as it makes you happy.

The Truth: The terrorists were happy to kill and be killed in Jihad.

3. Religion is not a matter of True vs. False, or good vs. evil. It is a matter of subjective personal choice.

The Truth: This statement refutes itself as it can be dismissed as someone's personal choice.

4. All religions are True. Thus, we must not judge other religions.

The Truth: Christianity is True when it says there is only one way to heaven, Jesus Christ. Our religion says to judge other religions. You cannot judge us and then pretend that you do not believe in judging others.

5. We must be tolerant of other views.

The Truth: Great! Then you must tolerate Jesus when He said to identify and reject False prophets. But if you do not tolerate Him, then you are intolerant.

6. Islam is a religion of peace.

The Truth: This is a lie. Both the Qur'an and the Hadith teach Muslims to destroy the lives and properties of those who will not accept Islam. This is called Jihad.

7. Jews and Christians fared better under Islam than in Christian lands.

The Truth: This is refuted by Bat Ye'or in *The Dhimmi: Jews and Christians Under Islam* (Fairleigh Dickinson University Press, 1985).

8. The Terrorists were not True Muslims.

The Truth: No? They are acting upon what the founder of Islam taught in the Hadith and what is found in the Qur'an. This is why they are called "Muslim Fundamentalists" as opposed to liberal Muslims who do not believe in the Qur'an or the Hadith. It is the liberals who are not True Muslims because they deny the teachings of the founder of the religion they claim to follow.

9. This is a war against terrorists and not against the religion of Islam.

The Truth: The U.S. cannot go to war against any religion. It can only fight nations and terrorist groups. But the terrorists have declared a religious Jihad against us. Their motivation is 100% religious. The ROOT is Islam while the FRUIT is terrorism.

Question #4—Since the Qur'an says in Surah 2:256 "Let there be no compulsion in religion," doesn't this mean that true Islam does not force its religion on others?

Answer: First, Surah 2 is a Meccan surah, which means that it was delivered while Muhammad was living in Mecca, while he only had a few followers. Later, when he moved to Medina, he gained enough followers to field an army. Once he had the ability to wage war, the prohibition against compulsion was abrogated by later Medinan verses and thus has no relevance for today.

Second, radical Isalm does not have the same idea of what constitutes "compulsion" as do Westerners. Waliyyuddin Shareef reveals how fundamentalist Muslims interpret the "no compulsion" passage:

> Mr. Morey also claims that Muhammad forced people to give up their idols and accept Islam. This statement is not true. What Muhammad did was give a choice to the pagans and idol worshippers to either give up their idols or die. No force was used, just a choice. If you believe in your idols, then are you willing to die for them is the question that was faced. I put this question to Mr. Morey and his readers: Are you willing to die for your belief in Jesus Christ?
>
> (In Response to Robert Morey's *Islamic Invasion*, p. 35.)

Question #5—Are the Arabs the descendents of Ishmael and thus the children of Abraham?

Answer: No, they are not the descendants of Ishmael or Abraham.

1. According to the Torah in Genesis 12, when Abraham left Ur of the Chaldees, he went West to what is now called Israel. He became a dweller in tents in that land. It was in Israel that God made a covenant with him for the land in which he was living at that time.

It was in Israel that he fathered Isaac, Ishmael and
many other sons and daughters. Isaac was the only son of
Abraham chosen by God to be the heir of the covenant.
Abraham took Isaac to Mount Moriah to be offered up as a
sacrifice to God.

2. The Torah is contradicted by the Qur'an at nearly
every point. According to Surah 2:119-121, Abraham and
Ishmael did not dwell in tents in Israel but in the city of
Mecca in Arabia. Together they rebuilt the Kabah and
placed the black stone in the wall. It was Abraham who
started the tradition of an annual pilgrimage to Mecca,
throwing stones at the devil, etc. Abraham took Ishmael
(not Isaac) to nearby Mount Mina to offer as a sacrifice to
God.

3. Ishmael's twelve sons were named Nebaioth, Kedar,
Adbeel, Mibsam, Mishma, Dumah, Massa, Hada, Tema,
Jetur, Naphish and Kedemah (Genesis 25:12-16). They
intermarried with the local population in North Arabia and
produced several nomadic tribes known as the
"Ishmaelites."

4. It was prophesied in the Torah that Ishmael and his
family would "live to the east of all his brothers" (Genesis
16:12). "And they settled from Havilah to Shur which is
east of Egypt as one goes toward Assyria" (Genesis 25:18).
This broad area is the desert section east of Egypt in
Northern Arabia toward the kingdom of the Assyrians.

5. The Ishmaelites are mentioned as a distinct tribe in
the Assyrian records. They later intermarried with and were
absorbed by the Midianites and other local tribes. In
Genesis 37:25-28 and 39:1, the Ishmaelites are called the
Midianites and in Judges 8:22-24 (cf. 7:1f), the Midianites

are called the Ishmaelites. The identification cannot be made any stronger.

6. Abraham came from Shem while the Arabs came from Ham. Thus, it is no surprise to find that Arabia was already populated by the descendants of Ham; i.e. the Arabs, long before Abraham or Ishmael were born (Genesis 10:7). Their cities and temples have been well documented by archeologists. At the time Ishmael was born, there were over a million Arabs in existence. This fact alone refutes the myth that Ishmael was the father of the Arabs.

7. If all the Arab people descended from Ishmael as Muhammad claimed, where did all of the original Arabs go? What happened to them? Who did Ishmael marry if the Arabs did not already exist? If Arabia was unpopulated, who built Mecca? Since he moved there, obviously it existed before he was born. The facts speak for themselves. The Arab people existed before, during and after Ishmael moved and started roaming the wilderness of North Arabia.

8. The descendants of Ishmael were scattered in Northern Arabia from the wilderness of Shur to the ancient city of Havilah. They were absorbed by the local tribes such as the Midianites (Genesis 37:25-28; 39:1; Judges 8:24).

9. There is no historical or archeological evidence that Ishmael went south to Mecca and became the Father of the Arab race. Modern Arab scholars admit that before Muhammad, Qahtan was said to be the Father of the Arab people, not Ishmael.

10. One Muslim scholar by the name of Shareef admitted in his book, *In Response To Robert Morey's Islamic Invasion*, that the pre-Islamic genealogies of Arab tribes do not list Ishmael as an ancestor.

"In pre-Islamic times Ishmael was never mentioned as the father of the Arabs" (p. 3).

Further documentation can be found in the references below.

"... Arabian literature has its own version of prehistoric times, but it is entirely legendary" (*Encyclopedia Britannica*, Volume 2:76).

"The pure Arabs are those who claim to be descended from Joktan or Qahtan, who the present Arabs regard as their principle founder.... The 'Arabu 'l-Musta'ribah, the mixed Arabs, claim to be descended from Ishmael.... They boast as much as the Jews of being reckoned the children of Abraham. This circumstance will account for the preference with which they uniformly regard this branch of their pedigree, and for the many romantic legends they have granted upon it.... The Arabs, in their version of Ishmael's history, have mixed a great deal of romance with the narrative of Scripture" (*A Dictionary of Islam*, pgs. 18-19).

"Muhammad was not informed about the family of Abraham" (*Encyclopedia of Islam*, I:184, also pages 544-546).

"There is a prevalent notion that the Arabs, both of the south and the north, are descended from Ishmael; and the passage in Genesis 16:12, 'He (Ishmael) shall dwell in the presence of all his brethren', is often cited as if it were a prediction of that national interdependence which, upon the whole, the Arabs have maintained more than any other people. But this supposition is founded on a misconception of the original Hebrew, which runs literally, 'he shall dwell before the faces of all his brethren'; i.e., (according to the idiom above explained, in which 'before the face' denotes the East), the habitation of his posterity shall be 'to the east' of the settlements of Abraham's other descendants.... These prophecies found their accomplishment in the fact of the sons of Ishmael being located, generally speaking, to the east of the other descendants of Abraham, whether of Sara or of Keturah.

"But the idea of the southern Arabs being of the posterity of Ishmael is entirely without foundation, and seems to have originated in the tradition invented by Arab vanity that they, as well as the Jews, are of the seed of Abraham. A vanity that, besides disfiguring and falsifying the whole history of the patriarch and his son Ishmael, has transferred the scene of it from Palestine to Mecca" (*Cyclopedia of Biblical, Theological, and Ecclesiastical Literature*, McClintock and Strong, Volume 1:339).

"The Ishmaelites are coupled with the Midianites" (*The Zondervan Pictorial Encyclopedia Of The Bible*, vol. 3, pgs.333-334).

In the Qur'an, "Genesis 21:17-21... is identified with Mecca" (*Concise Encyclopedia of Islam*, pg. 19).

The Southern Arabs come from Qahtan, not Ishmael (*Concise Encyclopedia of Islam,* page 48).

The connection between the Midianites and the Ishmaelites is noted (*The Encyclopedia of Religion*, Vol. 7, page 296).

See also: *The Shorter Encyclopedia of Islam,* pages 178-179.

A Popular Dictionary of Islam, page 127

Question #6—Where did the Qur'an come from?

Answer: Modern scholars, using sound principles of literary analysis, have determined that the Qur'an did not come from Muhammad. He did not recite it and actually never saw a copy of it. It was not put together in its present written form until nearly one hundred years after Muhammad's death.

This has come as quite a shock to Muslims. According to the legends, myths and stories found in the Hadith, the Qur'an was written in heaven by Allah on a large stone tablet. The angel Gabriel brought it down and Muhammad recited it verbally but did not write any of it down. It was Muhammad's companions who wrote down what he recited. After his death, it was gathered together and compiled by the Caliph Uthman.

The insurmountable problem that Muslims face is that they do not have any documentary evidence from the 7th or 8th century to back up any of their claims. For example, if Uthman compiled the Qur'an as the Hadith claims (Bukhari I:63; IV:709; VI:507, 510), where is the manuscript evidence for this? Why have no Qur'ans survived from that period? Why do we have to wait over a hundred years before we find even a scrap of the Qur'an?

The Muslims are also guilty of circular reasoning when they document the Qur'an by the Hadith and then document the Hadith by the Qur'an! But there is no documentary evidence to back up the Hadith or the Qur'an! They are both fraudulent as to authorship and dates.

Some Muslims have claimed that 7th century copies of the original Qur'an have been found in museums at Topkapi, Turkey and Tashkent, Russia. But when they were examined by manuscript scholars, they turned out to be 9th or 10th century manuscripts.

The Qur'an was invented in order to give spiritual unity to the vast empire created by Arab conquests. By borrowing liberally from the legends, myths and religious traditions of pagans, Jews, Christians, Hindus and Persians, they created one religion to rule over all its citizens. Thus, the Qur'an was the product of multiple authors from different times and places. These authors contributed stories and legends from their own cultural and religious background. The sources of these stories have been well documented by many scholars.

The burden of proof is now clearly on the Muslims. They must supply scholars with the documentary evidence to support their theories on the origins of the Qur'an and the Hadith. Until they do so, we cannot believe in the inspiration of either one.

How different is the situation with the New Testament! The manuscript evidence for it begins twenty years after the death (and resurrection) of Christ. There are literally thousands of Greek, Latin, Syriac and Coptic texts that document the reliability of the New Testament.

The same holds true for the historicity of Jesus of Nazareth. We have more than enough literary documentation for the life of Jesus from first century Jewish, pagan and Christian manuscripts. This is in sharp contrast to the life of Muhammad. We find no references to him as a prophet until 150 years after his death. No one has ever found even the smallest fragment of the Qur'an from the 7th century. Thus, much of what is said about the life of Muhammad must now be dismissed as fiction.

The truth will triumph in the end. The Qur'an and the Hadith were political tools used to subjugate non-Arab cultures by forcing them to accept as statutes of divine law a religion that elevated Arabian language, political laws, moral standards, dress codes, penal punishments and other cultural elements. This is why to become a Muslim you must take an Arab name, dress like an Arab, speak Arabic, eat only what Arabs eat, treat your wife as Arabs treat their wives, etc.

The religion of Islam was thus born out of Arab cultural imperialism and is rooted in a racist attitude that all things Arab are good while all things non-Arab are evil. Until this is understood, the true nature of Islam cannot be grasped.

This is why Western dress, food, movies, hairstyles, etc., are zealously denounced by the Mullahs and Imams as Satanic. Such things as blue jeans are not really condemned because they are immoral but because they are not Arab.

The truthfulness of this observation is easily demonstrated by Islam's demand that one bow in prayer in the direction of Arabia (Mecca) and make a pilgrimage to Arabia (Mecca). The religion of Islam is Arabian paganism and culture raised to divine law and imposed upon conquered nations.

Nations such as Egypt, Turkey, Lebanon, etc., who had the misfortune of having Islam forced upon them by the sword, need to break free from Arab imperialism in order to regain their own identity and culture. Until they throw off the shackles of Islam, they cannot become free societies where human rights are honored.

Question #7—Was Muhammad a black man or a white man? What was his view of the black man? Was he a slave master of black slaves?

Answer: These questions are very important for black Americans because they have been conned by Wallace D. Ford, Malcom X, Elijah Muhammad, Louis Farrakhan, Muhammad Ali, Mike Tyson and other "black" Muslims into thinking that Muhammad was a black man and Islam is the black man's religion. What is the truth?

First, Muhammad was a white man. There can be no doubt of this because the Hadith states this plain and simple. Since Bukhari is accepted by all Muslims as the greatest of all Hadith scholars, we will use his collection of

Hadiths. His work is entitled "Sahih" which means that it is
absolutely authentic.

In Hadith 1:63, when a man arrived at the mosque, he
asked, "Who amongst you is Muhammad?" The
companions of the prophet replied, "This white man
reclining on his arm."

Muhammad is described as "a white person" in Hadith
2:122. And in 2:141 when Muhammad raised his arms in
prayer, we are told, "the whiteness of his armpits became
visible."

In Hadith 1:367, we read that Anas, one of
Muhammad's most trusted companions, "saw the whiteness
of the thing of Allah's prophet" when his robe moved to the
side. While some Muslims, like Shabir Ally and Jamal
Badawi, argue over whether the "thing" refers to the thigh
or to the penis of Muhammad, they do not deny that it was
"white" whatever it was.

Any black man or woman who converted to Islam
because he or she was told that Muhammad was a black
man and thus Islam was the "black man's religion" should
now realize that he or she was suckered into becoming a
Muslim by lies and deception. The only thing he or she can
do to regain his dignity and to escape being a fool is to
renounce Islam.

Second, Muhammad was a slave owner of black
slaves. In Hadith vol. 6:436 when Umar came to visit
Muhammad, he saw "a black slave of Allah's apostle
sitting on the first step."

Lest some Muslim will claim that Muhammad had
only one black slave, we will now quote from Ibn Qayyim

al-Jawiyya, a great Muslim historian. In his famous book Zad al-Ma'ad (Part 1, pg. 160) we read:

> Muhammad had many male and female slaves. He used to buy and sell them, but he purchased more slaves than he sold, especially after God empowered him by His message, as well as after his immigration from Mecca. He once sold one black slave for two. His name was Jacob al-Mudbir.

This writer also tells us on pages 114-116 the names of Muhammad's black slaves: Bilal, Abu Hurairah, Usamah Ebn Zaayed and Rabbah were some of the black slaves of Muhammad. Among the black slaves was a black man by the name of Hahran. His story bears telling in the next section.

The most famous slave market was in Mecca during Muhammad's day. Black people stolen from African villages were auctioned off like cattle. This same slave market in Mecca was still being used for buying and selling black slaves until the late 1960's!

In the Sudan, as you read this material, the Muslim slave market has been revived as blacks in chains from the Dinka tribe are now being auctioned off to Muslim masters. (See *Islamic Invasion*, p. 199 for the documentation.) In Arabic, the common word for "Black" is "abd" which also means "slave".

In 1992, a book written by Jean Sasson shook the Muslim world. It was entitled *Princess* because it was the true story of a Saudi Princess in her own words. In her autobiography she revealed that her Muslim family had many black slaves. On page 29 we read:

"We owned a family of Sudanese slaves. Our slave population increased each year when Father returned from Haj, the annual pilgrimage to Mecca made by Muslims, with new slave children."

The Haj is the greatest religious event in all Islam. And what do the Muslims do on their Haj? Buy more black slaves!

Third, Muhammad mistreated his black slaves. It is clear that Muhammad treated his black slaves as animals of burden. The black slave Mahran tells us his story in his own words. The great Muslim historian, Ibn Qayyim al-Jawiyya, records that:

Mahran was renamed (by Muhammad) Safina (i.e., ship). He relates his own story. He says, "The apostle of God and his companions went on a trip. When their belongings became too heavy for them to carry, Muhammad told me, 'Spread your garment.' They filled it with their belongings, then they put it on me. The apostle of God told me, 'Carry it, for you are a ship.' Even if I were carrying a load of six or seven donkeys while we were on a journey, anyone who felt weak would throw his clothes or his shield or his sword on me so I would carry that, a heavy load. The prophet told me, 'You are a ship.'"

It does not take a Ph.D. to see that Muhammad mistreated Mahran and made him carry heavy loads. He even changed his name to "ship" to degrade him. The name "Safina" meant that the black slave Mahran was nothing more that a ship to carry Muhammad's burdens.

"But," one Muslim stated, "these are things from long ago. Islam does not make racist statements against blacks anymore." But Malik Ibn Ons, one of Islam's most respected modern scholars, states in his commentary on Muhammad's teachings on slavery:

> The master does not have the right to force the female slave to wed an ugly black slave if she is beautiful and agile unless in the case of utmost necessity (Ibn Hazm, vol. 6, Part 9, p. 469).

Referring to black men as "ugly black slaves" cannot be understood as anything less than racism.

In the Qur'an, Surah 33:50-52 tells us that a slave master could force sex upon his female slaves. The expression "those whom thy right hand possesses out of the prisoners of war" has always been interpreted by Muslim scholars to mean that a Muslim slave master could force his slaves to have sex with him.

Only the Day of Judgment will reveal how many black women were raped by Muslim masters. Since the Muslims were in the slave business long before they got the Europeans involved, and the Muslims are still enslaving and raping slaves today in black Africa, a fearful judgment awaits the Muslims.

Fourth, Muhammad was prejudiced against black people. He said that if you dreamed of black women, this was an evil omen (Hadith 9:162,163). He referred to black people as "raisin heads" (Hadith 1:662).

It has now been demonstrated from Muslim books that Muhammad was a white, a racist, a slave owner of black slaves who treated them as animals to carry his burdens, or as sex slaves. He enslaved blacks and treated them as animals. No intelligent black man or woman should have any respect for Muhammad or his racist religion.

Question #8—Does the Qur'an have scientific errors?

<u>Answer:</u> If the Qur'an is the infallible Word of God, then it stands to reason that it would not contain factual errors of science. By "factual errors" we mean errors that can be physically examined. We are not talking about contradictions between scientific theories and the Qur'an. We are talking about hard evidence that can be checked.

But first, there is a question we must answer: "Is it legitimate to judge the Qur'an?" Many Muslims believe in the Qur'an as a blind leap of faith. They really do not care if it is filled with mistakes and contradictions. As far as they are concerned, they were born Muslim and they will die Muslim. The more closed-minded they are, the more fanatical they become in their religion. When ignorance unites with arrogance, fanaticism is born.

We pity those whose religion is only the product of an accident of birth and culture. They blindly follow whatever religion they were born into. How sad it is to have an unexamined faith, a faith that cannot stand up to reason and science, a faith that merely shouts slogans, stamps its feet, and beats its breast in a mindless mob. They do not believe in Islam because it is true. To them Islam is true because they believe it.

> "A poor player that struts and frets his hour
> upon the stage and then is heard no more; It is a
> tale told by an idiot, full of sound and fury,
> signifying nothing" (Mac Beth, Act V, Scene 5).

Thankfully, there are millions of Muslims today who have received a university education and understand that an unexamined faith is a worthless faith. They are open-minded to scientific facts and evidence. They want the truth, the whole truth and nothing but the truth.

THE SETTING OF THE SUN

One of the questions that puzzled the ancient Arabs was, "Where did the sun go when night time came?" The Qur'an gave them Allah's answer:

He [i.e. Zul-qarnaim] followed, until he reached the setting of the sun. He found it set in a spring of murky water (Kahf Surah XVIII, vs. 85-86).

We agree with Muslim scholars that Zul-qarnain refers to Alexander the Great (see Yusuf Ali's appendix on this subject in his translation of the Qur'an). According to this surah, Alexander the Great traveled west until he found out what happened to the sun. It went down into and under the murky waters of a pond. When it was completely covered by the water, darkness fell upon the earth.

To the early Muslims, this surah gave the divine answer as to why darkness fell when the sun set in the West. They assumed that the sun like the moon was the size perceived by the human eye, about the size of a basketball. Darkness came when with a mighty hissing roar it went down under the dark waters of a pond. They boldly and proudly proclaimed that this marvelous answer proved that the Qur'an was indeed the Word of God.

Today, modern Muslims are quite embarrassed by this passage and try to ignore it or to quickly dismiss it as poetry. But the passage is not part of a poem. Thus it cannot be dismissed as figurative language or poetic license. In the context, it is part of a historical narrative that relates several historical incidents in the life of Alexander the Great.

The Qur'an's mistake was based on the erroneous assumption that the earth was flat. The authors of the Qur'an did not know that the earth was a sphere that revolved around the sun.

The reader must ask himself if he is prepared to believe and to defend the Qur'an in this passage. Either the sun sets in a pond or it doesn't. It is either one way or the other. There can be no middle ground, no compromise, no evading the issue. If you agree with us that the sun is shining on the other side of the earth and thus it does not go down into murky water, then you must also agree with us that the Qur'an contains scientific errors.

Question #9—What is the "Nation of Islam" that is headed by Louis Farrakhan?

Answer: One of the little known facts about the Muslim movement in the African-American community is that there are at least seven "Black" Muslim cults, each claiming to be the only "true" Nation of Islam. Obviously, either one of these cults is the "true" Nation, while the other six are frauds, or they are all frauds. But they cannot all be "the" Nation of Islam.

What they are fighting over is who is the "heir" to the bizarre teachings of Elijah Poole, better known by his alias, Elijah Muhammad. He was a semi-illiterate Southern black man who was a disciple of a white cult leader by the name of Wallace Dodd Ford.

The police record on W. D. Ford is quite long and includes drug dealing and other rackets. He left the drug business and decided to set up a new religion specifically designed to draw in angry, young black men who wanted to escape from the poverty and racism rampant in Northern cities such as Detroit, Chicago, D.C., L.A., and N.Y.C. By playing on the emotions of bitterness, despair and hate, Ford manipulated poor uneducated blacks to give him their souls as well as their money.

Not being knowledgeable about the Bible, Ford utilized the cultic teachings of another white man by the name of Charles Taze Russell, the founder of the Watchtower Bible and Tract Society, or as they are called today, the Jehovah's Witnesses. Ford combined Russellism with the teachings of the Moorish Science Temple, originally headed by Timothy Drew.

Ford changed his name frequently but is today known to his modern disciples as Master Fard Muhammad. He told his disciples that he was Allah (God) and thus they had to submit to his divine authority. To their shame they bought into his con game hook, line and sinker.

Ford also taught that there were 24 black men who were the original gods. The white race was created by a black god named Yakub. White men were created as devils and this explains why they have treated the black race with such disrespect. Due to the lies and tricks of these white devils, the Black man has forgotten that all Blacks are gods and goddesses.

These teachings are made all the more bizarre by the fact that Fard was a white man! Thus the Nation of Islam was founded by a white devil before whom black men bowed while calling him "Master" Fard Muhammad. We would laugh at such irony if not for the fact that the souls of thousands of black men and women were damned for all eternity by the false teachings of Fard.

Elijah Poole was a poor southern black who moved to Detroit in search of a better life, but all he found was crushing poverty and ruinous drunkenness. He was drawn to Ford's racist dogma that white people are devils as a way to excuse his own indolence. Instead of accepting responsibility for his own failures in life, Poole blamed the white man as the cause of all his ills. Blaming the white race for all the evils which afflict the Black man has proven to be the most successful bait on the hook to reel in new converts to this day.

Ford changed Poole's name to Kareem. But after Ford disappeared, Kareem changed his name to Muhammad. He went on to claim to be Allah just as Ford had done. The unquestioning devotion paid to him by his followers made it possible for him to have multiple adulterous affairs. Before long, a host of illegitimate children proved to be his undoing. After his death, the courts were besieged by women whose children had been sired by Elijah.

After Ford died, the Nation fell into at least seven competing sects. The most well known cult is the Farrakhanites who now proclaim that Louis Farrakhan is Allah. The 5% cult is another "Nation of Islam". It has had a field day with Farrakhan's "Million Man" March on Washington, D.C.

The 5%ers correctly point out that Elijah Muhammad said that the Muslims must never march on Washington, D.C. Thus Louis has lost all credibility so far as his claim that he is the heir of Elijah.

In the end, all the Nations will be shown by history to be frauds. By their denial of the Gospel, they have rejected the only hope for divine forgiveness and the only way to find true dignity and worth.

If you have been drawn into the web of Islam by Farrakhan, Wallace or the 5%ers, repent of your sins and turn to JESUS CHRIST for salvation. You are not a god, but a poor lost sinner in need of forgiveness and salvation. Break free from the mind control and brain washing used by the Nations of Islam. JESUS is the only Savior of sinners. Ford, Poole, Farrakhan and all other false gods will not help you on the Day of Judgment.

For a detailed examination of the history and teachings of the Nation of Islam, see Bishop Akridge's book, *Why I Am Not A Black Muslim,(1-800-41-TRUTH)*.

Question #10—Was Muhammad illiterate?

This may seem a strange question but the supposed "miracle" of the Qur'an hangs on the answer. If he could neither read or write, how did he read and recite the Qur'an that was brought down from heaven by Gabriel? It would take a miracle for him to do so.

While Muslims dogmatically assert that Muhammad was illiterate, when I checked their own historical writings, I found that Bukhari's Hadith records that he could, in fact, both read and write (Bukhari IV:393)! The so-called miracle of the Qur'an is dashed to the ground by the most reliable primary source material.

During one debate with a Muslim scholar, when I confronted him the documentation from his own writings that Muhammad was not illiterate, the Muslims in the audience began shouting the Arabic word for death!

PART TWO

HOW TO DEFEAT RADICAL ISLAM

CHAPTER EIGHT

IT IS TIME FOR TOUGH LOVE

America is at war whether we like it or not. The days to come do not bode well for the property and lives of Americans overseas or here at home. The specter of a nuclear and biological attack looms large on the horizon. Liberals are more concerned about protecting the feelings of Muslims than protecting the lives of Americans. If loyal Americans do not rise up and demand that the present government fulfill its constitutional duty to protect the lives and property of the citizens of this great land, who will?

This chapter will outline what has to be done internationally and nationally to win the war against Muslim terrorism. If we do not implement this plan, thousands, if not millions, will die.

THE FINAL SOLUTION TO INTERNATIONAL TERRORISM

Is there anything so important to Muslim terrorists such as bin Ladin, that in order to save it, they will renounce their Jihad against America? Is there anything so important to Saudi Arabia and other Muslim countries that in order to save it, they will stop supporting terrorism? Do we have any leverage in our war with radical Islam?

Since they are willing to commit suicide and to sacrifice their own family members to achieve their terrorist goals, it would seem that there is nothing so important to them that the mere thought of losing it would bring their Jihad to a halt. But this is not true.

The terrorists and terrorist nations such as Saudi Arabia only fear one thing: *the destruction of the religion of Islam*. There is nothing in this life that has greater value to them than Islam. They are willing to sacrifice and even die to promote Islam. This *religious* motivation is the engine that drives the Jihad against us.

THE ACHILLES HEEL OF ISLAM

The path to Paradise, according to the Five Pillars of Islam, involves the city of Mecca and its stone temple called the Kabah. Muslims pray toward Mecca five times a day. What *if Mecca didn't exist anymore?*

They must make a pilgrimage to Mecca and engage in an elaborate set of rituals centered around the Kabah once they arrive. *What if Mecca and the Kabah were only blackened holes in the ground?*

What if Medina, the burial place of Muhammad, was wiped off the face of the planet?

What if the Dome Mosque on the Temple site in Jerusalem was blown up?

The greatest weakness of Islam is that it is hopelessly tied to sacred cities and buildings. If these cities and buildings were destroyed, Islam would die within a generation as it would be apparent to all that its god could not protect the three holiest sites in Islam.

The Sword Held Over Their Heads

With American ships stationed all around Arabia and troops on the ground within Saudi Arabia itself, it would take about seven minutes for cruise missiles to take out Mecca and Medina. These cities could be vaporized in minutes and there is nothing that the Saudis or any other Muslim country could do to stop us. The Israelis could take out the Dome Mosque at the same time. It could happen so fast that no one would have the time to respond. With these surgical strikes, few lives would be lost. And, with three strikes against them, Islam is out!

The Threat

The US government and its allies must agree that this is the final solution to the Muslim problem. We must tell all terrorist groups that the next time they destroy the lives and property of Americans at home or abroad, we will destroy Mecca, Medina and Dome Mosque. They will be responsible for destroying the three most holy sites in Islam and bringing the religion to its knees.

We must tell all the Muslim countries that are presently supporting and harboring terrorists that if they do not cease and desist at once, we will destroy the heart of their religion.

Saudi Arabia and the rest of the Islamic World would, for the first time in their bloody history of oppression and tyranny, have to give civil rights and human rights to women and non-Islamic religions. They would have to allow their people to decide for themselves what religion, if any, they want in their lives. The "religious police" would be disbanded.

All Islamic laws would have to give way to the UN declaration on human rights, civil rights, women's rights and freedom of religion. Once Muslim governments took their foot off the neck of their people, millions of Muslims would convert to Christianity as they have had enough of oppression and violence from their Imams and Mullahs.

HOME SECURITY

What must we do to catch all the terrorists hiding in this country before they are activated and kill more Americans? Tough love demands that we act swiftly and without any concern for feelings. When people are dying, we do not have the luxury of political correctness. The following steps must be taken at once.

1. Education

No school, college or university that receives federal or state aid may register or teach any students who do not provide a birth certificate or the appropriate papers proving that they are legal citizens of this country. If a school, college or university refuses to comply with this requirement, all federal and state aid is to be suspended until they do.

Any students who fail to provide a birth certificate or the papers to prove they are legal immigrants, shall be turned over to the appropriate federal and state authorities to see if the entire family is illegal. If they are all illegal, they must be rounded up, interrogated and, unless they can show due cause, they should be sent back to their home country.

2. *Medical Services*

All hospitals and doctors must require patients to provide a birth certificate or the appropriate papers proving that they are legal citizens of this country. Since illegal aliens are not citizens, they do not have a right to free medical care. Any and all illegal aliens who apply for medical attention will be turned over to the appropriate federal and state authorities to see if the entire family is illegal. If they are all illegal, they must be rounded up, interrogated and, unless they can show due cause, they should be sent back to their home country.

3. *Draft Registration*

All males must register for the draft when they reach 18 years of age. At that time, they provide a birth certificate or the appropriate papers proving that they are legal citizens of this country. Any male who fails to provide a birth certificate or the papers to prove he is a legal immigrant, shall be turned over to the appropriate federal and state authorities to see if his entire family is illegal. If they are all illegal, they must be rounded up, interrogated and, unless they can show due cause, they should be sent back to their home country.

4. *Employment*

All employees must provide a birth certificate or the appropriate papers proving to their employers that they are legal citizens of this country. Any male who fails to provide a birth certificate or the papers to prove he is a legal immigrant shall be turned over to the appropriate federal and state authorities to see if his entire family is illegal. If they are all illegal, they must be rounded up, interrogated and, unless they can show due cause, they should be sent back to their home country.

5. Police Check Points

In addition to providing car registration and an insurance certificate whenever a vehicle is stopped for any reason, drivers shall also provide a birth certificate or the appropriate papers proving that they are legal citizens of this country. Any driver who fails to provide a birth certificate or the papers to prove he is a legal immigrant shall be turned over to the appropriate federal and state authorities to see if his entire family is illegal. If they are all illegal, they must be rounded up, interrogated and, unless they can show due cause, they should be sent back to their home country.

6. Bank and Stock Information

In addition to a valid Social Security number, any one seeking to open or maintain a bank account or to use any financial services must provide a birth certificate or the appropriate papers proving that they are legal citizens of this country. Anyone who fails to provide a birth certificate or the papers to prove he is a legal immigrant, shall be turned over to the appropriate federal and state authorities to see if his entire family is illegal. If they are all illegal, they must be rounded up, interrogated and, unless they can show due cause, they should be sent back to their home country.

7. Welfare and Unemployment Benefits

All those who apply for welfare or unemployment benefits must provide a birth certificate or the appropriate papers proving that they are legal citizens of this country.

Anyone who fails to provide a birth certificate or the papers to prove he is a legal immigrant, shall be turned over to the appropriate federal and state authorities to see if his entire family is illegal. If they are all illegal, they must be rounded up, interrogated and, unless they can show due cause, they should be sent back to their home country.

8. Immigration

Any citizens, students or illegal immigrants from Islamic countries that are listed by the State Department as being a terrorist state, must report for registration and interrogation. Anyone who fails to provide a birth certificate or the papers to prove he is a legal immigrant, shall be turned over to the appropriate federal and state authorities to see if his entire family is illegal. If they are all illegal, they must be rounded up, interrogated and, unless they can show due cause, they should be sent back to their home country.

9. Military Service

Since several terrorists received their training in the U.S. military, all Muslim military personal and Muslim chaplains must be deemed as a security risk and not allowed access to sensitive information or to weapons of mass destruction.

10. Mosques and Islamic Information Centers

All mosques and Islamic centers must provide all financial records of any and all funds sent outside of this country. If full disclosure reveals that a Mosque or an Islamic Center sent money to any terrorist cause or group, they are to be shut down as agents of a foreign power. In America, people are free to believe whatever they want.

But they are not free to seek the overthrow of the government or to destroy the property and lives of those who disagree with them.

11. The Intelligence Community

The FBI, the CIA, and other intelligence agencies of the United States shall be given full power to infiltrate Muslim charitable groups, mosques, schools and centers and to seek the identity of anyone who supports terrorism by any means deemed necessary.

CONCLUSION

If these ten measures are adopted and put into action, within two years America will be a safe place to live and work. If they are not adopted, then the terrorists will have the freedom to destroy the lives and property of Americans at will.

These steps will be taken now or later. Once a nuclear or bio-chemical holocaust is unleashed against America, people will be ready for tough love. But why wait until millions of Americans are dead or dying before doing what we all know must be done to protect this land?

CHAPTER NINE

PRIMARY DOCUMENTS

Introduction

The supporting documents given below are taken from the Qur'an and the Hadith, which are viewed by Muslim authorities as the "first" and "second" inspirations.

According to Muslim traditions, the Qur'an was written in pure Arabic in heaven by Allah on a large stone table. The angel Gabriel took the table of the Qur'an and made Muhammad recite it. His recitations were memorized or written down by others on whatever objects were on hand such as sticks, stones, bones, palm leaves, etc.

After Muhammad died, various conflicting Qur'ans were produced. It was the Caliph Uthman who made his own version of the Qur'an the official one (See Bukhari's Hadith vol. 1, pg. 56, no. 63). He later burned all the other conflicting Qur'ans. The Qur'an sold today is substantially the Uthman version.

The Hadith is the record of the teachings and example of Muhammad and his interpretations of the Qur'an. They are thus authoritative for all Muslims. To deny the Hadith is to be guilty of apostasy under Islamic Law. The greatest of all Hadith scholars was Bukhari.

Since most people do not have access to the Qur'an or the Hadith, we have supplied some of the material that is referred to in this book. For more details on the history of the Qur'an and the Hadith, see the books: *Islamic Invasion* (Christian Scholars Press) and *Muhammad's Believe It Or Else!* (Crescent Moon Publishers).

The Doctrine of Abrogation

Surah 2:106—None of our revelations do we abrogate or cause to be forgotten, but we substitute something better or similar.

Muslim Terms Used Before Islam

Surah 2:127-128 —And remember Abraham and Ishmael raised the foundations of the House (with this prayer)... "Our Lord! Make of us Muslims...." Surah 2: 132 —And this is the legacy that Abraham left to his sons, and so did Jacob: "Allah has chosen the Faith for you; then die not except in the Faith of Islam."

Jihad

Surah 2:190-194 —Fight in the cause of Allah against those who fight you... and kill them wherever you catch them.... If they fight you, kill them. Such is the reward of those who suppress the Faith.... And fight them on until there is no more tumult or oppression, and there prevail justice and faith in Allah.

Surah 2:216—Fighting is prescribed for you.

Surah 2:244—Fight in the cause of Allah.

Surah 4:74—Let those who fight in the cause of Allah, who sell the life of this world for the Hereafter, to him who fighteth in the cause of Allah.... Soon shall we give him a reward of great value.

Surah 4:89—If they turn apostates, seize them and kill them wherever you find them.

Surah 4:91—Seize them and kill them wherever you get them.

Surah 5:33—The punishment of those who wage war against Allah and his apostle...they shall be slaughtered, or crucified , or their hands and feet shall be struck off alternately, or they shall be banished from the land.

Surah 5:51—O ye who believe! Take not the Jews and the Christians for your friends.

On Jesus

Surah 5:72-73—They do blaspheme who say: Allah is Christ the son of Mary.... They do blaspheme who say: Allah is one of three (gods).... Christ the son of Mary was no more than an apostle.

Ask No Questions

Surah 5:101—Ask not questions about things which, if made plain to you may cause you trouble.... Some people before you did ask such questions, and on account lost their faith (in Islam).

The Greatest Deceiver

Surah 3:54 —The greatest Deceiver (Makara)
of them all is Allah.

Beating Wives

Surah 4:34—Men are the managers of the
affairs if women...those you fear may be rebellious
admonish; banish them to their couches, and beat
them.

Jews Turning into Monkeys, Rats and Pigs

The Qur'an

Surah 2:65—And you know well those
among you who transgressed in the matter of the
Sabbath: We said to them: "Become monkeys!
Despised and rejected."

Surah 7:163-166—Ask them about the town
which stood by the seashore. Behold! They sinned
in regard to the Sabbath. On their Sabbath day, the
fish swam up to them and stuck their heads out of
the water [to tempt the people to catch them]. But
the fish did not do this on the day that was not the
Sabbath. In this way We tempted them because
they were devoted to sinning. When some of them
said, "Why do you bother preaching to people
whom Allah will destroy or inflict with a terrible
punishment?" The preachers responded, "To fulfill
our obligation to their Lord and they might yet
fear Him." When they ignored the warnings given
to them, We saved those who avoided evil, but We

punished the evil-doers with a grievous
punishment because they were devoted to sinning.
When in their insolence they transgressed the
warnings, We said to them, "Become monkeys!
Despised and rejected."

The Hadith

Bukhari, vol. IV, chapter 32, p. 415 —The
statement of Allah: And ask them (O Muhammad)
about the town that was by the sea, when they
transgressed in the matter of the Sabbath. (1) when
their fish came to them only on the Sabbath day
and did not come..."Become monkeys! Despised
and rejected."

Bukhari, vol. IV, no. 524, pg. 333—The
Prophet said, "A group of Israelites were lost.
Nobody knows what they did. But I do not see
them except that they were cursed and
transformed into rats, for if you put the milk of a
she-camel in front of a rat, it will not drink it, but
if the milk of a sheep is put in front of it, it will
drink it."

(1)   It was illegal for the Israelites to eat
        the meat or drink the milk of camels
        while they were allowed to eat the
        meat and drink the milk of sheep. The
        prophet inferred from the rat's habit
        that some of the Israelites had been
        transformed into rats.

(2)   Later on the prophet was informed
        through Inspiration about the fate of
        those Israelites: They were
        transformed into pigs and monkeys.

A Test of Prophethood

<u>The Hadith</u>

Bukhari vol. IV. no 546—When Abdullah bin Salam heard of the arrival of the Prophet at Medina, he came to him and said, "I am going to ask you about three things which nobody knows except a prophet:

1. What is the first sign of the Hour (i.e. the end of the world)?

2. What will be the first meal taken by the people of Paradise?

3. Why does a child resemble its father and why does it resemble its maternal uncle?"

Allah's Apostle said, "Gabriel just now told me of their answers."

Abdullah said, "He (i.e., Gabriel), from amongst all the angels, is the enemy of the Jews."

Allah's Apostle said, "The first sign of the Hour will be a fire that will bring together the people from the East to the West; the first meal of the people of Paradise will be extralobe of fish-liver. As for the resemblance of the child to its parents: If a man has sexual intercourse with his wife and gets his discharge first, the child will resemble the father, and if the woman gets her discharge first, the child will resemble her."

The Seal of Prophethood

The Qur'an

Surah 33:40—Mohammed is not the father of any of your men, but (he is) the Apostle of Allah and the Seal of the Prophets (rests upon him).

The Hadith

Bukhari vol. I, no. 189; vol. no. 741—Narrated As-Sa'ib Yazid: ...I stood behind him (i.e., Allah's Apostle) and saw the Seal of Prophethood between his shoulders, and it was like the "zir-al-Hijla" (the size of a button on a small tent or a partridge egg).

Bukhari vol. IV, no. 741 Narrated As Sab'ib bin Yazid: ...standing behind him (i.e., Allah's Apostle) I saw the Seal (of the Prophets) between his shoulders."

Muslim vol. IV, no. 5790-5793

Chapter CMLXXIX—The Fact Pertaining to the Seal of His Prophethood, Its Characteristic Feature and Its Location on His Body.

Jabir b. Samura reported: "I saw the Seal on his back as if it were a pigeon's egg." This hadith has been narrated on the authority of Simak with the same chain of transmitters.

As-Sa'ib b. Yazid reported: My mother's sister took me to Allah's Messenger and ...I stood behind him and I saw the Seal between his shoulders.

Abdullah b. Sarjis reported: I saw Allah's Apostle and ate with him bread and meat.... I then went after him and

saw the Seal of Prophethood between his shoulders on the
left side of this shoulder having spots on it like moles.

The Story of a Giant She-Camel Prophet

The Qur'an

Surah VII:73—To the Thamud people ...This
she-camel of Allah is a sign unto you: So let her
graze on Allah's earth and do not let her come to
any harm, or you will be seized by a terrible
punishment.

Surah VII:77—Then they ham-strung the she-
camel and insolently defied the order of their
Lord...so the earthquake took them unawares and
they lay prostrate in their homes in the morning.

Surah LIV:23 —The Thamud rejected their
Warners.

Surah LIV:27—For We sent the she-camel as
a trial for them.

Surah LIV:29—But they called to their
companion and he took a sword in his hand and
ham-strung her.

Surah LIV:30-31—Ah! How terrible was my
penalty and my warning! For We sent against
them a single mighty blast and they became like
the dry stubble used by one who pens cattle.

Surah XCI:11—The Thamud people rejected
their prophets through their inordinate wrong-
doing.

Surah XCI:13-14—But the apostle of Allah said to them, "It is a she-camel of Allah! Do not hinder her from drinking." But they rejected him and ham-strung her. So their Lord, on account of this crime, destroyed the traces of them and made them all suffer equally.

The Companions of the Cave

The Qur'an

Surah XVIII:9-25—Do you understand that the Companions of the Cave and of the Inscription were wonders among our signs? Behold, the youths entered the Cave and said, "Our Lord, bestow upon us your mercy and deal with us in the right way." We drew a veil over their ears for a number of years in the Cave. Then we awakened them in order to test which of the two parties was best at calculating the number of years they had stayed in the Cave. We relate to you their story in truth.... So they stayed in their Cave three hundred years and some add nine more years to that.

The Man Who Died for a Hundred Years

The Qur'an

Surah II:259—Or take the similitude of one who passed by a village in ruins to its roofs. He said, "Oh! How shall Allah restore it to life after its death?" But Allah caused him to die for 100 years. Then he raised him up and said, "How long have you stayed here?" He said, "A day or a part

of a day." He said, "No, you have been here for
100 years! But look at your food and your drink,
they show no signs of age. And look at your
donkey! We have made you a sign unto the
people. Look further at the bones (of your body)
how We clothed them with flesh."

A 90-Foot Adam

The Hadith

Bukhari vol. IV, no. 543 —Narrated Abu
Huraira: The Prophet said, "Allah created Adam,
making him 60 cubits tall."

No Dogs or Cats Allowed!

The Hadith

Bukhari vol. IV, nos. 539—Narrated Abu
Talha: The Prophet said, "Angels do not enter a
house which has either a dog or a picture in it.

Bukhari vol. IV, no. 540—Narrated Abdullah
bib Umar: Allah's Apostle ordered that the dogs
should be killed.

Muslim vol. I, no. 551—Ibn Mughaffal
reported: The Messenger of Allah ordered killing
of the dogs, and then said: "What about them; i.e.,
other dogs?" and then granted concession to keep
the dog for hunting and the dog for the herd and
said: "When the dog licks the utensil, wash it
seven times and rub it with dirt the eighth time."

Muslim vol. I, no. 552—A hadith like this has been narrated from Shu'ba with the same chain of transmitters except for the fact that in the hadith transmitted by Yahya those words are: "He (the Holy Prophet) gave concession in the case of the dog for looking after the herd, for hunting and for watching the cultivated land," and there is no mention of this addition (i.e., concession in case of watching the cultivated lands) except in the hadith transmitted by Yahya.

Footnote # 486—The dog is one of the unclean beasts according to Islam and eating its flesh is forbidden and its keeping in the house as a pet is also prohibited for the Muslims. They have, however, been permitted to keep dogs for hunting, herding and watching.

Chapter DCXVIII—The Price of a Dog...and the Selling of a Cat Forbidden:

Muslim vol. III, no. 3803—Abu Mas'ud al-Ansari reported that Allah's Messenger forbade the charging of price of the dog.

Muslim vol. III, no. 3806—Khadji reported Allah's Messenger as saying: "The price of a dog is evil."

Muslim vol. III, no. 3808—Abu Zubair said: I asked Jabir about the price of a dog and a cat; he said, "Allah's Messenger disapproved of that."

Muslim vol. III, no. 3809—Ibn 'Umar reported Allah's Messenger giving command for killing dogs.

Muslim vol. III , no. 3810 Ibn 'Umar
reported: Allah's Messenger ordered us to kill
dogs and he sent men to the corners of Medina
that they (i.e., the dogs) should be killed.

Muslim vol. III, no. 3813—Abu Zubair heard
Jabir b. Abdullah saying: Allah's Messenger
ordered us to kill dogs and we carried out this
order so much that we also killed the dog coming
with a woman from the desert.... He said, "It is
your duty to kill the jet-black dog having two
spots, for it is the devil."

(See also Muslim vol. III, nos. 3814-3829)

Satan in the Nose Over Night

The Hadith

Bukhari vol. IV, no. 516 —"Satan stays in
the upper part of the nose all night."

Footnote (1)—We should believe that Satan
actually stays in the upper part of one's nose,
though we cannot perceive how, for this is related
to the unseen world of which we know nothing
except what Allah tells us through his Apostle
Mohammed.

Muslim vol. I, no. 462—Abu Huraira
reported: The Apostle of Allah said, "When any
one of you awakes from sleep and performs
ablution, he must clean his nose three times, for
the devil spends the night in the interior of his
nose."

Playing Chess Forbidden

The Hadith

Muslim vol. IV, no. 5612, Chapter
CMXLVI— It Is Prohibited To Play Chess:
Allah's Apostle said, "He who played chess is like
one who dyed his hand with the flesh and blood of
swine."

Non-Muslims Have Seven Intestines!

The Hadith

Muslim vol. III, nos. 5113 Chapter
DCCCLXII—A Believer Eats In One Intestine
Whereas A Non-Believer Eats In Seven Intestines

Ibn Umar reported Allah's Messenger as
saying that a non-Muslim eats in seven intestines
while a Muslim eats in one intestine (see also nos.
5114-5120).

Don't Pray Looking Up

The Hadith: Muslim vol. I, nos. 863—Chapter
CLXXIII:

It Is Forbidden To Lift One's Eyes Toward
The Sky in Prayer: Abu Huraira reported Allah's
Apostle as saying: "People should avoid lifting
their eyes towards the sky while supplicating in
prayer, otherwise their eyes would be snatched
away."

The Wondrous Wings of a Fly

The Hadith

Bukhari vol. IV, no. 537—Narrated Abu Huraira: The Prophet said, "If a house fly falls into the drink of anyone of you, he should dip it (into the drink) because one of its wings has a disease and the other wing has the cure (for that disease).

Bukhari vol. VII, no. 673—Narrated Abu Huraira: Allah's Apostle said, "If a fly falls in the vessel of any of you, let him dip all of it into the vessel and then throw it away, for in one of its wings there is a disease and in the other wing there is healing."

The Qur'an Forgotten by the Prophet

The Hadith

Bukhari vol. VI, no. 558—Narrated Aisha: Allah's Apostle heard a man reciting the Qur'an at night, and said, "May Allah bestow His mercy on him, as he has reminded me of such and such verses of such and such Suras, which I was caused to forget."

Bukhari vol. VI, no. 562—Narrated Aisha: The Prophet heard a reciter reciting the Qur'an in the mosque one night. The Prophet said, "May Allah bestow his mercy on him, as he has reminded me of such and such verses of such and such Suras, which I missed."

The Setting of the Sun

The Qur'an

Surah 18:86—When he (i.e., Zul-qarnain) reached the setting of the sun, he found that it set in a pond of murky water.

Mohammad Bewitched!

The Hadith

Bukhari vol. VII. no. 658—Narrated Aisha: A man called Labid bin al-A'sam from the tribe of Bani Zaraiq worked magic on Allah's Apostle until Allah's Apostle started imagining that he had done a thing that he had not really done.

Bukhari vol. VII, no. 660—Narrated Aisha: Magic was worked on Allah's Apostle so that he used to think that he had had sexual relations with his wives while he actually had not... "He is under the effect of magic."

Bukhari vol, VII, no. 661—Narrated Aisha: Magic was worked on Allah's Apostle so that he began to imagine that he had done something although he had not.

The Prophet Had Lice

The Hadith

Bukhari vol. IX, no. 130—One day the Prophet visited her (i.e., the wife of Ubada bin As-Samit) and she provided him with food and started looking for lice in his head.

Drinking Camel Urine

The Hadith

Bukhari vol. I, no. 234—The Prophet ordered them to go to the herd of camels and to drink their milk and urine.

The Crying Palm Tree

The Hadith

Bukhari vol. II, no. 41—Narrated Jabir bin Abdullah: The Prophet used to stand by a stem of a date-palm tree. When the pulpit was placed for him we heard the stem crying like a pregnant she-camel till the Prophet got down down from the pulpit and placed his hand over it.

Bukhari vol. IV, no. 783—Narrated Ibn Umar: The Prophet used to deliver his sermons while standing beside the trunk of a date-palm. When he had the pulpit made, he used it instead. The trunk started crying and the Prophet went to it, rubbing his hand over it (to stop its crying).

The Fingers of Life

The Hadith

Bukhari vol. I, no. 170—He put his hand in that pot and ordered the people to perform ablution from it. I saw the water springing out from underneath his fingers.

Bukhari vol. IV, no. 773—I saw water flowing from underneath his fingers.

Bukhari vol IV, no. 776—So he placed his hand in that pot and the water started flowing among his fingers like springs.

Shouting Food

The Hadith

Bukhari vol. IV, no. 779—...no doubt, we heard the meal glorifying Allah, when it was being eaten (by Allah's Apostle).

600 Wings

The Hadith

Bukhari vol. VI. no. 380—Mohammed has seen Gabriel with six hundred wings.

The Devil Urinates into the Ear

The Hadith

Bukhari vol. II, no. 245—If one sleeps and does not offer the prayer, Satan urinates in his ears. Narrated Abdullah: The Prophet said, "Satan urinated in his ears."

No Garlic or Onions Allowed

The Hadith

Bukhari vol. I, no. 812—What has been said about uncooked garlic or onion. And the statement of the Prophet: "Whoever has eaten garlic or onion because of hunger or otherwise should not come near our mosque" (see also nos. 813-815).

Bukhari vol. VII, no. 362—Narrated Abdul Aziz: It was said to Anas, "What did you hear the Prophet saying about garlic?" Anas replied, "Whoever has eaten garlic should not approach our mosque."

Bukhari vol. VII, no. 363—Narrated Jabir bin Abdullah: The Prophet said, "Whoever has eaten garlic or onion should keep away from us."

Yawning Comes from Hell

<u>The Hadith</u>

vol. IV, no. 509—Narrated Abu Huraira: The Prophet said, "Yawning is from Satan."

Hell-Fire for Women

<u>The Hadith</u>

Bukhari vol. I, no. 28—The Prophet said, "I was shown the Hell-fire and that the majority of its dwellers were women who were ungrateful."

Bukhari vol. I, no. 301—Allah's Apostle... said, "O women! Give alms, as I have seen that the majority of the dwellers of Hell-fire were you women.... I have not seen anyone more deficient in intelligence and religion than you."

Bukhari vol. II, no. 161—The Prophet then said..., "I also saw the Hell-fire and I had never seen such a horrible sight. I saw that most of the inhabitants were women."

No Assurance of Salvation

The Hadith

Bukhari vol. V, no. 266—The Prophet said, "By Allah, even though I am the Apostle of Allah, yet I do not know what Allah will do to me."

What Made the Prophet Afraid?

The Hadith

Bukhari vol. II, no. 167—The sun eclipsed and the Prophet jumped up, terrified that it might be the Hour [of Judgment].

Healing Palm Leaves

The Hadith

Bukhari vol. II, no. 443—The Prophet passed by two graves and those persons (in the graves) were being tortured.... He then took a green leaf of a date-palm tree, split it into two pieces and fixed one on each grave. The people said, "O Allah's Apostle! Why have you done so?" He replied, "I hope that their punishment may be lessened until they (i.e., the palm leaves) become dry."

What Color was Mohammed?

The Hadith

Bukhari vol. 1, no. 63—While we were sitting with the Prophet in the mosque, a man came riding on a camel. He made his camel kneel down in the mosque, tied its foreleg and then said, "Who among you is Mohammed?" At that time the Prophet was sitting among us leaning on his arm. We replied, "The white man reclining on his arm."

Bukhari vol. II, no. 122—Mohammed is described as "a white person."

Bukhari vol. II. no. 141—When the Prophet raised his arms in prayer "the whiteness of his armpits became visible."

Bukhari vol. IV, no. 744—Narrated Ismasil bin Abi Khalid: I heard Abu Juhaifa saying, "I saw the Prophet and Al-Hasan bin Ali resembled him." I said to Abu Juhaifa, "Describe him (i.e., Allah's Apostle) for me." He said, "He was white and his beard was black with some white hair in it. He promised to give us 13 young she-camels, but he died before we got them."

What Color Was the Apostle's Hair?

The Hadith

Bukhari vol. I, no. 167—About the dyeing of hair with henna: Without a doubt I saw Allah's Prophet dyeing his hair with it and that is why I like to dye my hair with it. (See also vol. IV, no. 747 and vol. VII, no. 785.)

A Child Bride

The Hadith

Bukhari vol. V, nos. 234—Narrated Aisha:
The Prophet was engaged to me when I was a girl
six years old.... I was playing in a swing with
some of my girl friends.... Unexpectedly Allah's
Apostle came to me in the afternoon and my
mother handed me over to him. At that time I was
a girl of nine years of age.

Bukhari vol V, no. 236—The Prophet...
married Aisha when she was a girl of six years of
age and consummated that marriage when she was
nine years old.

CONCLUSION

The primary documents speak for themselves. Non-
Muslims are astonished and stupefied that any sane person
would believe that, in the light of the absurd things he
taught, Muhammad was a prophet. Islam is no more
rational than it is peaceful.

Muslims are in a real bind at this point. They are
bound by Islamic Law to accept the inspiration of both the
Qur'an and the Hadith. If they try to save Muhammad by
rejecting the Hadith, they are not only apostates and
therefore subject to the death penalty, but they have pulled
the historical rug from underneath the Qur'an.

The above teachings of Mohammad have the same
chain of authorities as does the history of the text of the
Qur'an itself. The Hadith and the Qur'an stand or fall
together.

CHAPTER TEN

MUSLIM APOLOGISTS AND THEIR LOGICAL FALLACIES

When witnessing to Muslims, Christians must be prepared to answer the typical objections made against the Gospel. Most of the objections are based on simple logical fallacies. The following is a list of some of the most common fallacies expressed by Muslims.

1. Fallacy of False Assumptions

In logic as well as in law, "historical precedent" means that the burden of proof rests on those who set forth new theories and not on those whose ideas have been verified. The old tests the new. The established authority judges any new claims to authority.

Since Islam came along centuries after Christianity, Islam has the burden of proof and not Christianity. The Bible tests and judges the Qur'an. When the Bible and the Qur'an contradict each other, the Bible must logically be given first place as the older authority. The Qur'an is in error until it proves itself.

Some Muslims violate the principle of historical precedent by asserting that Islam does not have the burden of proof and that the Qur'an judges the Bible.

2. Arguing in a Circle

If you have already assumed in your premise what you are going to state in your conclusion, then you have ended where you began and proven nothing. For example, by proving Allah by the Qur'an and then proving the Qur'an by Allah, or by proving Muhammad by the Qur'an and then proving the Qur'an by Muhammad, or by proving Islam by the Qur'an and then proving the Qur'an by Islam, you have proved nothing.

3. False Analogy

Comparing two things as if they are parallel when they are not really the same at all. For example:

a. Many Muslims erroneously assume that Muslims and Christians share the same concepts of God, revelation, inspiration, textual preservation, the Bible, prophethood, biblical history, conversion, etc.

b. Because a false analogy is drawn between Islam and Christianity, some Muslims think that any argument that refutes the Qur'an will likewise refute the Bible; any argument which refutes Muhammad will also refute Jesus Christ, etc.

c. Many Muslims claim that Muhammad and all the prophets were sinless, even denying that Abraham was an idol worshipper.

Thus, when a Christian points out all the wicked things that Muhammad did (mass murder, child abuse, lying, etc.), the Muslims will say, "If you are right, then you must also reject your prophets for doing wicked things as well."

What the Muslims are really saying is, "If you reject our prophet, then you must reject your prophets as well. If Muhammad was a false prophet, then your prophets are false as well."

The root problem is that the Muslim concept of prophethood is not the same as the Christian concept of prophethood. We teach that prophets sin like anyone else. Thus, while Islam is refuted by the sins of Muhammad, Christianity is not jeopardized at all. The Muslim is guilty of setting up a "false analogy".

Whenever a Muslim responds to a Christian attack on the Qur'an, Muhammad or Allah by flipping the argument around and applying it to the Bible, Jesus or the Trinity—as if Islam and Christianity either stand or fall together—he is guilty of the fallacy of a false analogy; Islam can be false and Christianity be true at the same time.

4. The Fallacy of Irrelevance

When you introduce issues that have no logical bearing on the subject under discussion, you are using irrelevant arguments. For example, some Muslims argue, "The Qur'an is the Word of God because the text of the Qur'an has been preserved perfectly." This argument is erroneous for two reasons:

First, factually, the text of the Qur'an has not been preserved perfectly. The text has additions, deletions, conflicting manuscripts and variant readings like any other ancient writing.

Second, logically, it is irrelevant whether the text of the Qur'an has been preserved or not because preservation does not logically imply inspiration. A book can be perfectly copied without implying its inspiration.

When Muslims attack the character and motives of anyone who criticizes Islam, they are using irrelevant arguments. The character of someone is no indication of whether he is telling you the truth. Good people can lie and evil people can tell the truth. Thus, whenever a Muslim uses slurs such as "mean," "dishonest," "racist," "liar," "deceptive," etc., he is not only committing a logical fallacy but also revealing that he cannot intellectually defend his beliefs.

When confronted with the pagan origins of the Qur'an, some Muslims defend the Qur'an by answering, "But Christians celebrate Christmas and it was originally a pagan holiday! Thus both Muslims and Christians get their rites from the pagan." This argument is erroneous for several reasons.

> a. It is a false analogy to parallel the pagan origins of the rites commanded in the Qur'an with the present day holidays nowhere commanded in the Bible. What some modern-day Christians do on December 25th has no logical bearing on what the Qur'an commands Muslims to do (for example: the pilgrimage, the fast, etc.).

> b. It is irrelevant that some Christians choose to celebrate the birth of Christ. Since the Bible nowhere commands it, it is a matter of personal freedom. But Muslims are commanded in the Qur'an to believe and practice many things that came from the paganism of that day.

> c. The Muslim by using this argument is actually admitting that the Qur'an was not "sent down", but

fabricated from pagan sources. This means he has become an unbeliever (Surah 25:4-6).

Some Muslims argue that the Qur'an is the Word of God because it contains some historically or scientifically accurate statements. This argument is irrelevant. Just because a book is correct on some historical or scientific point does not mean it is inspired. You cannot take the attributes of a part and apply it to the whole. A book can be a mixture of true and false statements. Thus it is a logical fallacy to argue that the entire Qur'an is true if it makes one true statement.

When a Muslim argues that history or science "proves" the Qur'an, this means that he acknowledges that history and science can likewise refute the Qur'an. If the Qur'an contains just one historical or scientific error, then the Qur'an is not the Word of God. Verification and falsification go hand in hand.

The present meaning of a word is irrelevant to what it meant in ancient times. The word "Allah" is a good example. When confronted by the historical evidence that the word was used by pagan Arabs in pre-Islamic times to refer to a high god who was married to the sun goddess and had three daughters, some Muslims will quote dictionaries, encyclopedias, etc., to prove that "Allah means God." They are thus using modern definitions to define what the word meant over 1000 years ago! What "Allah" means now has no bearing on what it meant before Muhammad.

5. The Fallacy of Equivocation

If we assume that everyone has the same definition of such words as God, Jesus, revelation, inspiration, prophet, miracle, etc., we are committing a very simple logical fallacy.

When a Muslim says, "Christians and Muslims worship the same God," he is committing the fallacy of equivocation. While Christians worship the Triune God of Father, Son and Holy Spirit, Muslims worship a unitarian deity. Obviously, they are worshipping different gods.

When Muslims say, "We believe in Jesus, too", they are committing the fallacy of equivocation. The Jesus of the Qur'an is not the Jesus of the Bible. Islam preaches "another Jesus" (II Corinthians 11:4).

The Jesus of the Bible is God the Son who died on the cross for our sins. But the "Jesus" of the Qur'an is not God the Son, and he did not die on the cross for our sins. Thus, it is erroneous for Muslims to tell Christians that they believe in Jesus too.

When a Muslim assumes that Christians have the same concept of revelation as Muslims, he is guilty of the fallacy of equivocation. To Islam, the Qur'an was written in heaven by Allah and has no earthly source. When we prove that it comes from earthly sources, this threatens the inspiration of the Qur'an.

On the other hand, the Bible does not claim that it dropped out of heaven one day. It openly quotes from earthly sources. It uses pre-existing sources without any difficulty whatever. Thus, while the Qur'an is threatened by historical sources, the Bible is actually confirmed by them!

When a Muslim tells you that the word "Allah" has only one meaning, "the one true universal God", this is a logical fallacy. "Allah" has many different meanings:

a. It can be used as generic term like the English word, "god." Thus it can be applied to any god or goddess regardless if a true or false god is in view (Example: The "Allahs" of Hinduism).

b. The Nation of Islam uses "Allah" to refer to Wallace Dodd Ford, Elijah Muhammad and Louis Farrakhan, and teaches that all black people are "Allahs".

c. It has been used by some Christians in Arabic speaking countries as a generic name for God.

d. It was used in pre-Islamic times by pagan Arabs to refer to the moon god who was the father of al-Lat, al-Uzza, and Manat.

e. It is used by Muslims to refer to their god. Islam and Christianity do not worship the same God. The Christian worships the Holy Trinity while the Muslim worships a unitarian deity.

6. The Fallacy of Force

The Qur'an commands Muslims to wage war against non-Muslims and apostates (Surah 5:33; 9:5, 29). Some Muslims use a false analogy to answer this argument. They respond by saying, "Well, what about the Crusades? You Christians use violence just like Muslims." It is logically erroneous to set up a parallel between Muslims killing people in *obedience* to the Qur'an and Christians killing people in *disobedience* to the Bible. While the Qur'an commands Jihad, the New Testament forbids it.

7. *Confusing Questions of Facts and Questions of*
   Relevance

Whether something is factually true is totally different
from the issue of whether or not it is relevant. The two
issues must be kept separate. For example, when a
Christian argues that most of the stories, beliefs and rituals
of the Qur'an came from pre-Islamic Arab paganism, the
Muslim will deny it at first. But as more and more evidence
is given, the Muslim will often do a flip-flop and begin
arguing. "So what! Didn't you Christians get Christmas
from the pagans?" The Muslim has now committed three
fallacies.

The "So what?" argument is dealing with the issue of
relevance, not fact. You must stop the Muslim at that point
and ask him, "Since you are now dealing with the issue of
whether the pagan origins of the Qur'an are relevant, does
this mean that you are now agreeing to the fact of the pagan
origins of Islam?"

The Muslim has also committed the fallacy of
equivocation. The Bible is not threatened by historical
sources. It freely refers to them and even quotes them (Acts
17:28). But the Qur'an denies that it has any earthly
historical sources (Surah 25:4-6).

The Muslim also commits the fallacy of false analogy.
The Bible and the Qur'an are two totally different books.
The inspiration of the Bible does not depend upon the fate
of the Qur'an because what Muslims claim for the Qur'an
is not what Christians claim for the Bible.

8. Phonic Fallacies

The phonetic sound of a word should not be used to twist its meaning. For example:

a. Some Muslims try to prove that the word "Allah" is in the Greek New Testament because of the Greek word "alla."   But while the word is pronounced "allah", it only means "but" in Greek. It has nothing to do with the Arabic "Allah."

b. Some Muslims such as Deedat have claimed that the word "Allah" is in the Bible because of the biblical word "Allelujah." They then mispronounce the word as "Allah-lujah"! But "Allelujah" is not a compound Arabic word with "Allah" being the first part of the word. It is a Hebrew word with the name of God being "JAH" (or YAHWEH) and the verb "alle" meaning "praise to." It means "praise to YAHWEH." The Arabic word "Allah" is not in the word.

c. The same error is found in the Muslim argument that the word "Baca" (Psalm 84:6) really means "Mecca." They begin pronouncing "Baca," and then proceed it as "Baca-Maca-Mecca." But the Valley of Baca is in northern Israel and has nothing to do with the Arabian city of Mecca.

d. Some Muslims have even tried to go from "Amen" to "Ahmed" to "Muhammed"! Nonsense beyond belief!

9. "Red Herring" Arguments

When a Muslim is asked to defend the Qur'an, if he turns around and attacks the reliability of the Bible, the Trinity, the deity of Christ, the Crusades, etc., he is introducing irrelevant issues that have no logical bearing on the truthfulness of Islam. He is trying to divert attention from Islam to other issues.

Furthermore, he is assuming that if he can refute the Bible, then the Qur'an wins by default. If he can refute the Trinity, then Allah wins by default. But this is logically erroneous. You cannot prove your position by refuting someone else's position. The Bible and the Qur'an could both be wrong. Muslims must prove their own book.

10. Straw Man Arguments

When you put a false argument into the mouth of your opponent and then proceed to knock it down, you have only created a "straw man" argument. Muslims sometimes either misunderstand or deliberately misquote the arguments Christians give them.

For example, some Muslims claim that we teach, "The Qur'an teaches that Allah is the moon god and that Muslims knowingly believe in and worship the moon god and his daughters." They then knock down this "straw man" argument and claim victory.

Of course, we never said such nonsense. What we have said is that while the Qur'an claims that Allah is God and Muslims think they are worshipping the one true God, in reality they are worshipping a false god preached by a false prophet according to a false book.

CONCLUSION

The average Muslim has been deceived by Muslim apologists who use such logical fallacies without regard to reason, fact or honesty. But be patient. There are many Muslims who want to be rational in their religion and thus have an open mind to rational discourse. Once they see that their arguments are based on logical fallacies, they will be open to the wonderful news that Jesus Christ, the Son of God, rose from the dead and is coming again soon.

CONCLUSION

We can hear the screams of irate Muslims and confused liberals as they read this book. But we frankly do not care if we hurt their feelings. People are dying and it is time for tough love.

We care more about the future of America and Western civilization than political correctness. The final solution to the Muslim problem will require courage and commitment from this present generation of Americans. If we falter in our resolve to do whatever it takes to stop the terrorists, this nation is doomed.

We must also point out that to reward the terrorists by adopting their religion is repugnant to the rational mind. Now is not the time for inane relativism and sloppy universalism. All religions are not the same. All religions are not true. Islam is a violent and false religion. It cannot be transformed into a peaceful ideology simply by wishing it to be so. Facts are facts and they have the rude habit of smashing the delusions and dreams of idealists.

We have demonstrated that Islam is built upon three falsehoods: a false god, a false prophet and a false book. To say otherwise is to fly in the face of sound scholarship. It is our hope that we will destroy Mecca and Medina before a nuclear device is exploded in some American city. Why wait until hundreds of citizens are dead or dying from radiation poisoning? We must act now before Islamic terrorism gets to that stage.

APPENDIX

REPLY TO SHABIR ALLY

BY DR. ROBERT MOREY

INTRODUCTION

I have had the honor of having Muslim terrorists follow me around. In Canada, they threw acid at a car in which they thought I was riding. In Texas, they broke into a church building where they thought I was hiding. In San Diego, the FBI foiled an assassination attempt on my life. One Muslim even infiltrated my ministry and the FBI had to remove him.

Sometimes, terrorists show up at my lectures and protest outside the building or they run inside in an effort to disrupt my lecture. These are examples of terrorism. But at this time, thankfully, the goal is only character assassination. Lately, they have been giving out a booklet entitled: *"A Reply To Dr. Robert Morey's Moon-God Myth & Other Deceptive Attacks On Islam"* by Shabir Ally. Since I defeated Shabir in a public debate in Toronto, Canada (contact Faith Defenders, P.O. Box 7447, Orange, CA 92863 to obtain a video of this debate), it is obvious to me that this booklet is an *emotional* response to my book, *Islamic Invasion*. This is self-evident from his using such *ad hominem* slurs as "deceptive" and "dishonest." His booklet was an attack on me personally!

Let every Muslim terrorist please take note of the fact that I, Robert Morey, did not invent the idea that Allah came from Il or Ilah. Nor did I invent the idea that Allah in pre-Islamic times can be traced back to the Moon-God. Even if I had never been born, those ideas would have been voiced by many scholars and can be found in many reference works. This means that I am not personally your enemy. So, please stop running around like Shabir shouting insults at me. The emotionalism displayed in his booklet is "full of sound and fury, signifying nothing."

Shabir argues most of the time about irrelevant points that have nothing to do with the issue at hand. In logic, this is called the "red herring" fallacy. In order to stop the hounds from following the trail of their prey, someone would drag a smelly old red herring across the trail and the dogs would be led astray on a false trail.

This is Shabir's main logical fallacy. For example, instead of focusing on the crucial issues raised in the citations I give, he spends his time dealing with whether I quoted enough of the passage to suit him or whether I used … before or after the quote. In other words, Shabir wastes a great deal of time focusing on HOW I quoted a scholar instead of WHAT that scholar said. He is clearly guilty of using a red herring to divert people from WHAT I quoted. The rule of logic is: *The validity of what is quoted does not depend on whether … is placed before or after it or whether the entire passage is quoted.*

In my many books, lectures and debates, I set forth the following points:

1. In Pre-Islamic times, "Allah" was used by pagan Arabs in reference to one of 360 gods worshipped at the Kabah.

2. This "Allah" may have been a high god or even the top deity among the gods but he was not viewed in the monotheistic sense as the only true deity.

3. Many scholars trace this "Allah" back to Il and Ilah and from there to the Moon-God.

Do these points seem difficult to understand? I don't think so. The only crucial question is whether these points are supported by the citations I produce. It is irrelevant whether I quoted the entire paragraph or whether I put ... before or after the quote. If what I quoted supports the point I am making at the time, that is all that matters.

Since my points concern the *pre*-Islamic origin and meaning of "Allah," what it meant in *post*-Islamic times is *logically* irrelevant. Shabir seems completely ignorant of this point of logic.

He also doesn't understand that it is only necessary to quote that part of a page or paragraph or sentence that applies directly to the point you are making. Thus when Shabir constantly whines, "Morey did not quote the whole passage," he fails to understand that if the rest of the passage is irrelevant to the point being made, I don't have to quote it.

The same is true of Shabir's focus on if I used ... enough times to suit him. Yet, he failed to use... when quoting me on several occasions! The point is: The presence or absence of ... in a citation has no logical bearing on the validity of what is quoted.

Shabir's canard is immediately evident at this point. Take his treatment of my citation from Coon who wrote:

"The god Il or Ilah was originally a phase of the Moon God."

Carleton S. Coon, Southern Arabia, (Washington, D.C. Smithsonian, 1944) p. 399.

I used Coon to illustrate that some scholars trace "Allah" back to Il or Ilah. Then from there, they find its *original* meaning in pre-Islamic times to refer to the Moon-God. That this is what Coon is saying is quite clear. Now, why does Shabir object to my quotation from Coon?

1. He claims that I "misquoted" Coon. But did I in fact misquote him? No. He quotes the *exact same words* that I quoted! We both quote Coon's statement that the word Ilah originally referred to a phase of the Moon-God.

2. What Shabir means by "misquotation" is actually "*partial* quotation." He thus confuses partial quotation for misquotation. This is sad as it reveals he has no command of the English language or the laws of logic.

3. Thus Shabir's whole argument is based on the idea that since I did not quote the *whole* paragraph, this somehow means that what I did quote should be ignored! This is irrational.

After tracing Allah back to Il or Ilah and from there to the Moon-God, Coon goes on to discuss his idea of how

iv

the meaning of the word evolved *later on* in history. For example he states,

> "... under Mohammed's tutelage, the relatively anonymous Ilah, became Al-Ilah, The God, or Allâh, the Supreme Being."

Notice that Coon says that "under Muhammad's tutelage" (i. e., in *post*-Islamic times), "the relatively anonymous Ilah *became* Al-Ilah, the God, or Allah, the Supreme Being."

Read his words very carefully. Coon is saying that Muhammad *changed* the meaning of Allah. Coon says that the *original* meaning of Allah goes back to Il and from there back to the Moon-God. That the meaning of Allah was later CHANGED by Muhammad is further proof that Allah did NOT originally mean the only true God. After all, if it *changed* to the Supreme God, then it did not originally have that meaning!

Shabir makes the same mistake with my quote from Caesar Farah:

> "There is no reason, therefore, to accept the idea that Allâh passed on to the Muslims from the Christians and Jews" (Farah, p. 28).

Shabir once again confuses partial quotation with misquotation. He claims that I was in error for not quoting more of Farah. Well, here is the rest of Farah's statement:

> Allâh, the paramount deity of pagan Arabia, was the target of worship in varying degrees of intensity from the southernmost tip of Arabia to the Mediterranean. To the Babylonians he was "Il" (god); to the Canaanites, and later the Israelites, he was "El"; the South Arabians

v

worshipped him as "Ilah," and the Bedouins as "al-Ilah" (the deity). <u>With Muhammad he *becomes* Allâh, God of the Worlds</u>, of all believers, the one and only who admits no associates or consorts in the worship of Him. Judaic and Christian concepts of God abetted the <u>*transformation* of Allâh from a pagan deity to the God of all monotheists.</u> There is no reason, therefore, to accept the idea that "Allah" passed to the Muslims from Christians and Jews (Farah p. 28) (Emphasis mine).

Shabir does not realize that rather than refuting me, the expanded quotation actually supports what I say!

1. Farah begins by saying that Allah was the "paramount deity of pagan Arabia" and "a pagan deity." This means Allah was one of the gods worshipped by the pagans. Notice that he says "deity" and not "Deity."

2. Farah then clearly states that "with Muhammad" Ilah "BECOMES Allah," in that Allah is "TRANSFORMED" from being "a pagan deity" to a monotheistic Being. Again, this is what I also believe.

3. According to Farah, Allah began as a pagan deity and is later "transformed" by Muhammad into a monotheistic deity. This is the point I have been making all along.

The expanded quotes from both Coon and Farah support what I believe. The red herrings used by Shabir are revealed as a sham and a hoax. He should have focused on what I quoted and not just on how I quoted it.

The word Allah was most likely derived from *al-ilah* which had become the generic term for whatever god was considered the highest god. The Meccan pagans used *Allah* to refer to their own particular high god. This is why they prayed to Hubal using the name Allah. Different tribes preferred other names such as Sin or Ilqamah. Allah was NEVER called YHWH or Jesus.

The following citations reveal that there is a general consensus among Islamic scholars that Allah was a pagan deity before Islam developed in the 7th century. He was only one god among a pantheon of 360 gods worshipped by the Arabs. Even if he was at times viewed as a "high god," this does not mean he was the one true God.

"Allah: Originally applied to the moon; he seems to be preceded by Ilmaqah, the moon god....

Allat: the female counterpart to Allah."

Dictionary of Non-Classical Mythology, p. 7

"Allah: Before the birth of Muhammad, Allah was known as a supreme, but not sole, God."

Oxford Dictionary of World Religions, p. 48

"Before Islam, the religions of the Arabic world involved the worship of many spirits, called jinn. Allah was but one of many gods worshiped in Mecca. But then Muhammad taught the worship of Allah as the only God, whom he identified as the same God worshiped by Christians and Jews."

A Short History of Philosophy, (Oxford
University Press) p. 130

"Historians like Vaqqidi have said Allah was
actually the chief of the 360 gods being worshipped in
Arabia at the time Mohammed rose to prominence. Ibn Al-
Kalbi gave 27 names of pre-Islamic deities.... Interestingly,
not many Muslims want to accept that Allah was already
being worshipped at the Ka'ba in Mecca by Arab pagans
before Mohammed came. Some Muslims become angry
when they are confronted with this fact. But history is not
on their side. Pre-Islamic literature has proved this."

G. J.O. Moshay, *Who Is This Allah?* ,
(Dorchester House, Bucks, UK, 1994), pg.
138.

"Islam also owes the term 'Allah' to the heathen
Arabs. We have evidence that it entered into numerous
personal names in Northern Arabia and among the
Nabateans. It occurred among the Arabs of later times, in
theophorous names and on its own."

Ibn Warraq, *Why I Am Not A Muslim*,
(Prometheus, Amherst, 1995) p. 42.

"In any case it is an extremely important fact that
Muhammad did not find it necessary to introduce an
altogether novel deity, but contented himself with ridding
the heathen Allah of his companions subjecting him to a
kind of dogmatic purification."

Encyclopedia of Religion and Ethics, I:664

"The name Allah, as the Qur'an itself is witness, was well known in pre-Islamic Arabia. Indeed, both it and its feminine form, Allat, are found not infrequently among the theophorous names in inscriptions from North Africa."

Arthur Jeffrey, ed., *Islam: Muhammad and His Religion*, (New York: The Liberal Arts Press, 1958), p. 85.

"Allah is a proper name, applicable only to their [Arabs'] peculiar God."

Encyclopedia of Religion and Ethics, I:326.

"Allah is a pre-Islamic name...."

Encyclopedia of Religion and Ethics, I:117.

"Allah is found...in Arabic inscriptions prior to Islam."

Encyclopedia Britannica, I:643.

"The Arabs, before the time of Muhammad, accepted and worshipped, after a fashion, a supreme god called Allah."

Encyclopedia of Islam, eds. Houtsma, Arnold, Basset, Hartman (Leiden: E.J. Brill, 1913), I:302.

"Allah was known to the pre-Islamic Arabs; he was one of the Meccan deities."

Encyclopedia of Islam, ed. Gibb, I:406.

"Ilah…appears in pre-Islamic poetry…. By frequency of usage, al-ilah was contracted to allah, frequently attested to in pre-Islamic poetry."

> *Encyclopedia of Islam,* eds. Lewis, Menage, Pellat, Schacht (Leiden: E.J. Brill, 1971), II:1093.

"The name Allah goes back before Muhammed."

> *The Facts on File: Encyclopedia of World Mythology and Legend,* ed. Anthony Mercatante (New York, *The Facts on File*, 1983), I:41.

"The source of this (Allah) goes back to pre-Muslim times. Allah is not a common name meaning "God" (or a "god"), and the Muslim must use another word or form if he wishes to indicate any other than his own peculiar deity."

> *Encyclopedia of Religion and Ethics*, (ed. Hastings), I:326.

"Allah was already known by name to the Arabs."

> Henry Preserved Smith, *The Bible and Islam: or, The Influence of the Old and New Testament on the Religion of Mohammed,* (New York: Charles Scribner's Sons, 1897), p. 102.

"Allah: Perceived in pre-Islamic times as the creator of the earth and water, though not, at that time, considered monotheistically....

Allat: Astral and tutelary goddess. Pre-Islamic.... One of three daughters of Allah."

Encyclopedia of Gods, p. 11.

"Manat: Goddess. Pre-Islamic.... One of the so-called daughters of Allah."

Encyclopedia of Gods, p. 156.

"The name Allah is also evident in archeological and literary remains of pre-Islamic Arabia."

Kenneth Cragg, The Call of the Minaret,
(New York: Oxford University Press, 1956),
p. 31.

"In recent years I have become increasingly convinced that for an adequate understanding of the career of Muhammad and the sources of Islam great importance must be attached to the existence in Mecca of belief in Allah as a "high god". In a sense this is a form of paganism, but it is so different from paganism as commonly understood that it deserves separate treatment."

William Montgomery Watt, Muhammad's Mecca, p. vii.

"The use of the phrase 'the Lord of this House' makes it likely that those Meccans who believed in Allah as

xi

a high god – and they may have been numerous – regarded the Ka'ba as his shrine, even though there were images of other gods in it. There are stories in the Sira of pagan Meccans praying to Allah while standing beside the image of Hubal."

William Montgomery Watt, *Muhammad's Mecca*, p. 39.

"The customs of heathenism have left an indelible mark on Islam, notably in the rites of the pilgrimage (on which more will be said later), so that for this reason alone something ought to be said about the chief characteristics of Arabian paganism.

"The relation of this name, which in Babylonia and Assyria became a generic term simply meaning 'god', to the Arabian Ilah familiar to us in the form Allah, which is compounded of al, the definite article, and Ilah by eliding the vowel 'i', is not clear. Some scholars trace the name to the South Arabian Ilah, a title of the Moon god, but this is a matter of antiquarian interest…it is clear from Nabataen and other inscriptions that Allah meant 'the god'.

"The other gods mentioned in the Quran are all female deities: Al-Lat, al-Uzza, and Manat, which represented the Sun, the planet Venus, and Fortune, respectively; at Mecca they were regarded as the daughters of Allah…As Allah meant 'the god', so Al-Lat means 'the goddess'."

Alfred Guilaume, *Islam*, (Penguin, 1956) pgs. 6-7.

"As well as worshipping idols and spirits found in animals, plants, rocks and water, the ancient Arabs believed in several major gods and goddesses whom they considered to hold supreme power over all things. The most famous of these were Al-Lat, Al-Uzza, Manat and Hubal. The first three were thought to be the daughters of Allah (God) and their intercessions on behalf of their worshippers were therefore of great significance.

"Hubal was associated with the Semitic god Ba'al and with Adonis or Tammuz, the gods of spring, fertility, agriculture and plenty.... Hubal's idol used to stand by the holy well inside the Sacred House. It was made of red sapphire but had a broken arm until the tribe of Quraysh, who considered him one of their major gods, made him a replacement in solid gold.

"In addition to the sun, moon and the star Al-Zuhara, the Arabs worshipped the planets Saturn, Mercury, and Jupiter, the stars Sirius and Canopies and the constellations of Orion, Ursa Major and Minor, and the seven Pleiades.

"Some stars and planets were given human characters. According to legend, Al-Doberman, one of the stars in the Hades group, fell deeply in love with Al-Thruways, the fairest of the Pleiades stars. With the approval of the Moon, he asked for her hand in marriage."

Chair al-Sash, *Fabled Cities, Princes & Jin From Arab Myths and Legends,* (New York: Chicken, 1985), p. 28-30.

"Along with Allah, however, they worshipped a host of lesser gods and 'daughters of Allah.'"

Encyclopedia of World Mythology and Legend, I:61.

"It must not be assumed that since Moslems worship one God they are very close to Christians in their faith. The important thing is not the belief that God is One, but the conception that the believers have of God's character. Satan also believes and trembles! As Raymond Lull, the first great missionary to Moslems, pointed out long ago, the greatest deficiency in the Moslem religion is in its conception of God...For as we know, Jehovah the God of the Bible, known both to Jews and Christians, is revealed much differently than Allah, the god of Islam."

> Howard F. Vos, Ed., *Religions in a Changing World*, (Chicago, 1961), pp. 70, 71.

"Allah was the name of a god whom the Arabs worshipped many centuries before Muhammed was born."

> *The World Book Encyclopedia*, (Chicago, 1955), Vol. 1, p. 230.

"But history establishes beyond the shadow of doubt that even the pagan Arabs, before Mohammed's time, knew their chief god by the name of Allah and even, in a sense, proclaimed his unity.... Among the pagan Arabs this term denoted the chief god of their pantheon, the Kaaba, with its three hundred and sixty idols."

> Samuel M. Zwemer, *The Moslem Doctrine of God*, (New York, 1905), pp. 24-25.

"There is no corroborative evidence whatsoever for the Qur'an's claim that the Ka'aba was initially a house of monotheist worship. Instead there certainly is evidence as far back as history can trace the sources and worship of the Ka'aba that it was thoroughly pagan and idolatrous in content and emphasis."

John Gilchrist, *The Temple, The Ka'aba, and The Christ*, (Benoni, South Africa, 1980), p. 16.

"In pre-Islamic days, called the Days of Ignorance, the religious background of the Arabs was pagan, and basically animistic. Through wells, stones, caves, springs, and other natural objects man could make contact with the deity.... At Mekka, Allah was the chief of the gods and the special deity of the Quraish, the prophet's tribe. Allah had three daughters: Al-Uzzah (Venus) most revered of all and pleased with human sacrifice, Manah, the goddess of destiny, and Al Lat, the goddess of vegetable life. Hubal and more than 300 others made up the pantheon. The central shrine at Mekka was the Kaaba, a cube-like stone structure which still stands though many times rebuilt. Imbedded in one corner is the black stone, probably a meteorite, the kissing of which is now an essential part of the pilgrimage."

John Van Ess, *Meet the Arab*, (New York, 1943), p. 29.

"...a people of Arabia, of the race of the Joktanites...the Alilai living near the Red Sea in a district where gold is found; their name, children of the moon, so called from the worship of the moon, or Alilat."

Gesenius Hebrew and Chaldee Lexicon to the Old Testament Scriptures, translated by Samuel Prideaux Tregelles (Grand Rapids, MI, 1979), p. 367.

"That Islam was conceived in idolatry is shown by the fact that many rituals performed in the name of Allah were connected with the pagan worship that existed before Islam. And today, millions of Moslems pray towards Mecca, where the famous revered black stone is located.

"Before Islam, Allah was reported to be known as:

- the supreme of a pantheon of gods.

- the name of a god whom the Arabs worshipped.

- the chief god of the pantheon.

- Ali-ilah, the god, the supreme.

- the all-powerful, all-knowing, and totally unknowable.

- the predeterminer of everyone's life (destiny).

- the chief of the gods.

- the special deity of the Quraish.

- having three daughters: Al Uzzah (Venus), Manah

"...Because the rituals involved with the Islamic Pilgrimage are either identical or very close to the pre-Islamic pagan idol worship at Mecca. Because of other Arabian history which points to heathen worship of the sun, moon, and the stars, as well as other gods, of which I believe Allah was in some way connected to.

"This then would prove to us that Allah is not the same as the true God of the Bible whom we worship, because God never changes."

M. J. Afshari, Is Allah the Same God as the God of the Bible? pp. 6, 8, 9.

"If a Muslim says, 'Your God and our God is the same,' either he does not understand who Allah and Christ really are, or he intentionally glosses over the deep-rooted differences."

Adb-Al Masih, Who is Allah in Islam?
(Villach, Austria, Light of Life, 1985), p. 36.

"Sin. – The moon-god occupied the chief place in the astral triad. Its other two members, Shamash the sun and Ishtar the planet Venus, were his children. Thus it was, in effect, from the night that light had emerged…In his physical aspect Sin - who was venerated at Ur under the name of Nannar - was an old man with a long beard the color of lapis-lazuli. He normally wore a turban. Every evening he got into his barque -- which to mortals appeared in the form of a brilliant crescent moon -- and navigated the vast spaces of the nocturnal sky. Some people, however, believed that the luminous crescent was Sin's weapon. But one day the crescent gave way to a disk, which stood out in the sky like a gleaming crown. There could be no doubt that this was the god's own crown; and then Sin was called 'Lord of the Diadem.'

"These successive and regular transformations lent Sin a certain mystery. For this reason he was considered to be 'He whose deep heart no god can penetrate'… Sin was also full of wisdom. At the end of every month the gods came to consult him and he made decisions for them... His wife was Ningal, 'the great Lady'. He was the father not only of Shamash and Istar but also of a son Nusku, the god of fire."

Larousse Encyclopedia of Mythology, (New York, 1960), pp. 54-56.

"Allah, the Supreme Being of the Mussulmans: Before Islam. That the Arabs, before the time of Muhammed, accepted and worshipped, after a fashion, a supreme god called Allah, -- "the Ilah," or the god, if the form is of genuine Arabic source; if of Aramaic, from Alaha, "the god" -- seems absolutely certain. Whether he was an abstraction or a development from some individual god, such as Hubal, need not here be considered...But they also recognized and tended to worship more fervently and directly other strictly subordinate gods...It is certain that they regarded particular deities (mentioned in 1iii. 19-20 are al-'Ussa, Manat, or Manah, al-Lat; some have interpreted vii, 179 as a reference to a perversion of Allah to Allat as daughters of Allah, vi. 100; xvi. 59; xxxvii. 149; liii. 21); they also asserted that he had sons (vi. 100)... 'There was no god save Allah.' This meant, for Muhammed and the Meccans, that of all the gods whom they worshipped, Allah was the only real deity. It took no account of the nature of God in the abstract, only of the personal position of Allah...ilah, the common noun from which Allah is probably derived..."

First Encyclopedia of Islam, E.J. Brill (New York, 1987), p. 302.

"Islam for its part ensured the survival of these pre-Islamic constituents, endowed them with a universal significance, and provided them with a context within which they have enjoyed a most remarkable longevity. Some of these significant constituents, nomadic and sedentary, the pre-Islamic roots which have formed the persistent heritage, deserve to be noted and discussed...The pre-Islamic Pilgrimage in its essential features survives, indeed is built into the very structure of Islam as one of its Five Pillars of Faith."

The Cambridge History of Islam, Vol. I, ed.
P.M. Holt (Cambridge, 1970), p.27.

"The Quran (22.51/I) implies that on at least one occasion 'Satan had interposed' something in the revelation Muhammad received, and this probably refers to the incident to be described. The story is that, while Muhammad was hoping for some accommodation with the great merchants, he received a revelation mentioning the goddesses al-Lat, al-Uzza, and Manat (53.19 {20, as now found}), but continuing with other two (or three) verses sanctioning intercession to these deities. At some later date Muhammad received a further revelation abrogating the latter verses, but retaining the names of the goddesses, and saying it was unfair that God should have only daughters while human beings had sons."

The Cambridge History of Islam, Vol. I, ed.
P.M. Holt (Cambridge, 1970), p. 37.

"This notation at times might be very simple, as can be illustrated by such equations as the sun or winged sun for the sun-god (Sumerian, Utu; Akkadian, Shamash), a crescent moon for the moon-god (Nanna/Sin), a star for Inanna/Ishtar (the planet Venus), seven dots or small stars for the constellation Pleiades (of which seven are readily visible, or 'Seven Sisters')...."

Civilizations of the Ancient Near East, Vol.
III, ed. Jack M. Sasson, (New York), p.
1841.

"...the Ka'aba was dedicated to al-Ilah, the High God of the pagan Arabs, despite the presiding effigy of Hubal. By the beginning of the seventh century, al-Ilah had become more important than before in the religious life of many of the Arabs. Many primitive religions develop a belief in a High God, who is sometimes called the Sky God...But they also carried on worshipping the other gods, who remained deeply important to them."

Karen Armstrong, *Muhammad*, (New York:
San Francisco, 1992), p. 69.

"The cult of a deity termed simply "the god" (al-ilah) was known throughout southern Syria and northern Arabia in the days before Islam – Muhammad's father was named 'Abd Allah' ("Servant of Allah") – and was obviously of central importance in Mecca, where the building called the Ka'bah was indisputably his house. Indeed, the Muslims shahadah attest to precisely that point: the Quraysh, the paramount tribe of Mecca, were being called on by Muhammad to repudiate the very existence of all the other gods save this one. It seems equally certain that Allah was not merely a god in Mecca but was widely regarded as the "high god," the chief and head of the Meccan pantheon, whether this was the result, as has been argued, of a natural progression toward henotheism or of the growing influence of Jews and Christians in the Arabian Peninsula...Thus Allah was neither an unknown nor an unimportant deity to the Quraysh when Muhammad began preaching his worship at Mecca."

The Oxford Encyclopedia of the Modern Islamic World, ed. John L. Esposito, (New York, 1995), pp. 76-77.

"The religion of the Arabs, as well as their political life, was on a thoroughly primitive level...In particular the Semites regarded trees, caves, springs, and large stones as being inhabited by spirits; like the Black Stone of Islam in a corner of the Ka'bah at Mecca, in Petra and other places in Arabia stones were venerated also...Every tribe worshipped its own god, but also recognized the power of other tribal gods in their own sphere...Three goddesses in particular had elevated themselves above the circle of the inferior demons. The goddess of fate, al-Manat, corresponding to the Tyche Soteira of the Greeks, though known in Mecca, was worshipped chiefly among the neighboring Bedouin tribes of the Hudhayl. Allat – "the Goddess," who is Taif was called ar-Rabbah, "the Lady," and whom Herodotus equates with Urania – corresponded to the great mother of the gods, Astarte of the northern Semites; al-'Uzza, "the Mightiest," worshipped in the planet Venus, was merely a variant form...In addition to all these gods and goddesses the Arabs, like many other primitive peoples, believed in a God who was creator of the world, Allah, whom the Arabs did not, as has often been thought, owe to the Jews and Christians...The more the significance of the cult declined, the greater became the value of a general religious temper associated with Allah.

Among the Meccans he was already coming to take the place of the old moon-god Hubal as the lord of the Ka'bah...Allah was actually the guardian of contracts, though at first these were still settled at a special ritual locality and so subordinate to the supervision of an idol. In particular he was regarded as the guardian of the alien guest, though consideration for him still lagged behind duty to one's kinsman."

History of the Islamic Peoples, Carl Brockelmann, (New York), pp. 8-10.

"The Romans and Abyssinians were identified with Christianity. Whole tribes and districts held up the banner of Judaism and waged war in its propagation. The Persian power was the exponent of the fire-worship; and the Arabs in general were devoted to that native idolatry which had its center in the national sanctuary of the Kaaba...The religion most widely prevalent in Arabia, when Mohammed began his life, was a species of heathenism of idol-worship, which had its local center in Mecca and its temple...According to a theory held by many, this temple had been sourceally connected with the ancient worship of the sun, moon and stars, and its circumambulation by the worshippers had a symbolical reference to the rotation of the heavenly bodies. Within its precincts and in its neighborhood there were found many idols, such as Hobal, Lat, Ozza, Manah, Wadd, Sawa, Yaghut, Nasr, Isaf, Naila, etc. A black stone in the temple was regarded with superstitious awe as eminently sacred...The attempt of the Mussulmans to derive it direct from a stone altar or pillar, erected by Abraham and his son Ishmael, in that identical locality, is altogether unsupported by history, and, in fact, flagrantly contrary to the Biblical record of the life of Abraham and his son. The pagan character of the temple is sufficiently marked by the statement of Mohammedan writers that before its purification by their Prophet, it contained no less than 360 idols, as many as there were days of the year; and that on its walls were painted the figures of angels, prophets, saints, including those of Abraham and Ishmael, and even of the Virgin Mary with her infant Son...Mohammed, with great practical insight and shrewdness, seized on this advantage and retained the heathen shrine of his native city as the local center of Islam. He sanctioned it by his own example as a place of religious pilgrimage for all his followers."

Mohammed and Mohammedanism, S. W.
Koelle, (London, 1889), p. 17-19

"According to D. Nielsen, the starting point of the religion of the Semitic nomads was marked by the astral triad, Sun-Moon-Venus, the moon being more important for the nomads and the sun more important for the settled tribes."

Studies on Islam, trans., ed. Merlin L.
Swartz, (New York, Oxford, 1981), p.7.

"One detail which already impressed the Greek authors was the role played by sacred stones...The material object is not venerated for itself but rather as the dwelling of either a person being (god, spirit) or a force."

Studies on Islam, ibid., p. 8.

"The final divinity to be considered is Allah who was recognized before Islam as god, and if not as the only god at least as a supreme god. The Quran makes it quite clear that he was recognized at Mecca, though belief in him was certainly more widespread....How is this to be explained? Earlier scholars attributed the diffusion of this belief solely to Christian and Judaic influences. But now a growing number of authors maintain that this idea had older roots in Arabia...If, therefore, Allah is indigenous to Arabia, one must ask further: Are there indications of a nomadic source? I think there are, based on a comparison of the beliefs of the nomads in central and northern Asia with those of northeastern Africa. Like the supreme being of many other nomads, Allah is a god of the sky and dispenser of rain."

Studies on Islam, ibid., p. 12.

"The ibex (wa'al) still inhabits South Arabia and in Sabean times represented the moon god. Dr. Albert Jamme believes it was of religious significance to the ancient Sabeans that the curved ibex horn held sideways resembled the first quarter of the moon."

Qataban and Sheba: Exploring the Ancient Kingdoms on the Biblical Spice Routes of Arabia, Wendell Phillips, (New York, 1955), p. 64.

"The first pre-Islamic inscription discovered in Dhofar Province, Oman, this bronze plaque, deciphered by Dr. Albert Jamme, dates from about the second century A.D. and gives the name of the Hadramaut moon god Sin and the name Sumhuram, a long-lost city...The moon was the chief deity of all the early South Arabian kingdoms – particularly fitting in that region where the soft light of the moon brought the rest and cool winds of night as a relief from the blinding sun and scorching heat of day.

"In contrast to most of the old religions with which we are familiar, the moon god is male, while the sun god is his consort, a female. The third god of importance is their child, the male morning star, which we know as the planet Venus....

"The spice route riches brought them a standard of luxurious living inconceivable to the poverty-stricken South Arabian Bedouins of today. Like nearly all Semitic peoples they worshipped the moon, the sun, and the morning star. The chief god, the moon, was a male deity symbolized by the bull, and we found many carved bulls' heads, with drains for the blood of sacrificed animals."

Qataban and Sheba: Exploring the Ancient Kingdoms on the Biblical Spice Routes of Arabia, ibid. p. 227.

"Arabia in Muhammad's time was polytheistic in its conception of the cosmos and tribal in its social structure. Each tribe had its own god(s) and goddess(es), which were manifest in the forms of idols, stones, trees, or stars in the sky."

Islamic Studies, A History of Religions Approach, 2nd Ed., Richard C. Martin, (New Jersey), p. 96.

"II. The Religion of the Pre-Islamic Arabs

"The life of the pre-Islamic Arabs, especially in the Hijaz depended on trade and they made a trade of their religion as well. About four hundred years before the birth of Muhammad one Amr bin Lahyo bin Harath bin Amr ul-Qais bin Thalaba bin Azd bin Khalan bin Babalyun bin Saba, a descendant of Qahtan and king of Hijaz, had put an idol called Habal on the roof of the Kaba. This was one of the chief deities of the Quraish before Islam. It is said that there were altogether three hundred and sixty idols in and about the Kaba and that each tribe had its own deity...The shapes and figures of the idols were also made according to the fancy of the worshippers. Thus Wadd was shaped like a man, Naila like a woman, so was Suwa. Yaghuth was made in the shape of a lion, Yauq like a horse and Nasr like a vulture...Besides Hodal, there was another idol called Shams placed on the roof of the Kaba...The blood of the sacrifical animals brought by the pilgrims was offered to the deities in the Kaba and sometimes even human beings were sacrificed and offered to the god...Besides idol-worship, they also worshipped the stars, the sun and the moon."

Muhammad the Holy Prophet, Hafiz
Ghulam Sarwar (Pakistan), p. 18-19.

"The Bedouin do not seem to have had much time for religion. They were realists, without a great deal of imagination. They believed the land was peopled by spirits, the jinns, who were often invisible but appeared also in animal form. The dead were thought to live on in a dim and ghostly state. Offerings were made to them, and stelae and cairns of stones were erected on their graves. Certain trees and stones (especially meteorites and those shaped to resemble human forms) housed spirits and divinities. Divinities dwelt in the sky and some were actually stars. Some were thought to be ancient sages made divine. The list of these divine beings, and above all the importance with which each was regarded, varied from one tribe to the next; but the chief of them were to be found all over the peninsula. This was especially true of Allah, 'the God, the Divinity', the personification of the divine world in its highest form, creator of the universe and keeper of sworn oaths. In the Hejaz three goddesses had price of place as the 'daughters of Allah'. The first of these was Allat, mentioned by Herodotus under the name of Alilat. Her name means simply 'the goddess', and she may have stood for one aspect of Venus, the morning star, although Hellenized Arabs identified her with Athena. Next came Uzza, 'the all-powerful'; whom other sources identify with Venus. The third was Manat, the goddess of fate, who held the shears which cut the thread of life and who was worshipped in a shrine on the sea-shore. The great god of Mecca was Hubal, an idol made of red cornelian…Homage was paid to the divinity with offerings and the sacrifice of animals and perhaps, occasionally, of human beings. Certain sanctuaries were the object of pilgrimage (hajj) at which a variety of rituals were performed, consisting notably of ceremonial processions around the sacred object. Certain prohibitions had to be observed during these rituals, such as in many cases abstention from sexual relations. Magic was common. People feared the evil eye and protected themselves with amulets."

Mohammed, Maxine Robinson, (New York), pp. 16-17.

"These and many other verses show clearly that the existence of a god called Allah and even his highest position among the divinities was known and acknowledged in Jahiliyyah, but He was, after all, but one of the gods…Was the Koranic concept of Allah a continuation of the pre-Islamic one, or did the former represent a complete break with the latter? Were there some essential – not accidental – ties between the two concepts signified by one and the same name? Or was it a simple matter of a common word used for two different objects?

"In order to be able to give a satisfactory answer to these initial questions, we will do well to remember the fact that, when the Koran began to use this name, there immediately arose serious debates among the Arabs of Mecca. The Koranic usage of the word provoked stormy discussions over the nature of this God between the Muslims and the Kafirs, as is most eloquently attested by the Koran itself.

"What does this mean from the semantical point of view? What are the implications of the fact that the name of Allah was not only known to both parties but was actually used by both parties in their discussion with each other? The very fact that the name of Allah was common to both the pagan Arabs and the Muslims, particularly the fact that it gave rise to much heated discussion about the concept of God, would seem to suggest conclusively that there was some common ground of understanding between the two parties. Otherwise there could have been neither debate nor discussion at all. And when the Prophet addressed his adversaries in the name of Allah, he did so simply and solely because he knew that this name meant something – and something important – to their minds too. If this were not so, his activity would have been quite pointless in this respect.

"As regards the 'basic' meaning of Allah, …In pre-Islamic times each tribe, as a rule, had its own local god or divinity known by a proper name. So, at first, each tribe may have meant its own local divinity when it used an expression equivalent in meaning to 'the God'; this is quite probable. But the very fact that people began to designate their own local divinity by the abstract form of 'the God' must have paved the way for the growth of an abstract notion of God without any localizing qualification and then, following this, for a belief in the supreme God common to all the tribes. We meet with similar instances all over the world.

"Before the name [Allah] came into Islam, it had already long been part of the pre-Islamic system, and a considerably important part, too...the pagan concept of Allah, which is purely Arabian – the case in which we see the pre-Islamic Arabs themselves talking about 'Allah' as they understood the word in their own peculiar way."

God and Man in the Koran, Toshihiko
Izutsu, (Tokyo, 1964), pp. 95-99, 103-104.

One must ask why Shabir did not deal with all the citations I have given to prove my point? Could it be they are too clearly on my side?

SHABIR AND LOGIC

During our debate, I constantly pointed out the logical fallacies committed by Shabir. This must have irritated him greatly as he desperately tried to find a logical fallacy in my arguments.

First, I have argued that the word "Allah" existed before Muhammad was born. To prove this point, I pointed out that Muhammad's father and uncle both had "Allah" as part of their names. This is a historical argument that deals with the chronological reality that a father pre-exists his son. It would look like this:

If x exists before y,

Then: the father of Muhammad (x) existed before Muhammad (y).

If the name of x exists before the birth of y,

Then the name abd-Allah existed before the birth of Muhammad,

Then the word "Allah" existed before Muhammad.

I also build on this argument:

If x lived and died before y was born,

Then the meaning of x's name will be pre-y.

If the meaning of x's name is pre-y,

And x was a pagan,

Then the pre-y meaning of the name of x is pagan.

If "Allah" was part of x's name,

Then "Allah" is pre-y.

If the pre-y meaning of "Allah" was a pagan deity,

Then the name of x referred to a pagan deity.

If "Allah" came from Il or Ilah in pre-y times,

And Il or Ilah was originally the Moon-God,

Then Allah originally referred to the Moon-God.

In logic this last syllogism would be as follows:

$$a > b$$
$$\underline{b > c}$$
$$a > c$$

Shabir needs someone who teaches logic to tell him that the syllogism above is valid. He needs someone to tell him that logic deals with the validity of the form of an argument and not with whether the premise is true or false. Shabir does not understand this point. He assumes that because he denies the truth of my premise, this means my conclusion is invalid.

This is the fatal flaw of Shabir's entire booklet. He assumes a post-Islamic meaning of the word "Allah" as a reference to the one true deity of Islam. Thus, he resists any attempt to find a pagan pre-Islamic meaning of the word. He assumes Islam is true and then judges everything pre-Islamic by Islam.

Concerning the archeological evidence I set forth, Shabir cannot make up his mind. Sometimes he seems to deny it all and then in other places, he seems to admit that I was right. He contradicts himself on this point.

Shabir's main objection is a question of relevance and not fact. In some places he admits that I am right on the archeological facts but then turns around and claims that these facts are irrelevant. Thus it does not matter to him that Moon-God religion was dominant in the Fertile Crescent. But the cultural and religious context of the Pre-Islamic world in general is relevant because I am discussing that time period!

The fact is that Moon-God worship was the dominant religion in the ancient World. I surveyed the archeological evidence from Babylon to Egypt to prove this point. But Shabir complains,

"He should get to the point of proving that Moon-worship existed in Arabia."

Notice he says "Arabia" in general and not just Southern Arabia. He later condemns me for referring to Arabia in general. He thus does here what he later condemns me for doing.

After that, I pointed out that Moon-God temples have been found in Arabia and I quoted from scholars to prove this point. Does he deny that I am correct on this point? No.

How does Shabir try to wiggle out of the evidence I give? He commits the logical fallacy of *arguing from silence*. He asks, "But where is the evidence concerning North Arabia?" Since he can't deny the evidence that I submit, he just keeps asking for *more* evidence!

I set forth the hard evidence that moon worship was common among Pre-Islamic pagans in Arabia. He admits that this is true for Southern Arabia. But he waves this evidence away because archeologists have not been to

Northern Arabia. But modern archeologists are not allowed by the Saudis to dig in Northern Arabia. I am sure that such evidence would come to light if they were allowed to investigate the area.

The bulk of Shabir's booklet commits the same logical fallacies over and over again. When I quoted from Segall or other scholars that moon religion was dominant in Arabia, he complains that the evidence only proves this for Southern Arabia. But he waves aside this evidence by complaining the evidence has not been found in Northern Arabia.

He points to Minoan inscriptions that list names for the Moon-God and concludes that since Allah is not mentioned, this means it was not a name for the Moon-God. Of course, he is arguing from silence once again. It is logically irrelevant if a Minoan inscription does not mention the Arabic word Allah.

The depth to which Shabir now sinks is amazing. While every Islamic reference work defines Al-Lat, Al-Uzza and Manat as three pagan goddesses who were called the "daughters of Allah" by pagan Arabs in Pre-Islamic times, Shabir claims that I "invented" the idea that they were thus the daughters of the "Moon-God."

My conclusion that Al-Lat, Al-Uzza and Manat were viewed as the daughters of the Moon-God, is a valid deduction given the fact that Allah was originally the Moon-God in pre-Islamic times. The connection between Allah and the Moon-God has been pointed out by various scholars long before I came along. For example, *The Dictionary of Non-Classical Mythology*, states, "Allah: Originally applied to the moon..." (p. 7).

$$a > b$$
$$b > c$$
$$\underline{c > d}$$
$$a > d$$

Now, did I invent the statement above? No. Does Shabir set forth any citations to back up his denial of *The Dictionary of Non-Classical Mythology*? No.

I refer to "amazing discoveries" revealed by G. Caton Thompson in her 1944 book *The Tombs and Moon Temple of Hureidha*. What did she reveal? She uncovered a temple to the Moon-God in Southern Arabia. This is sufficient to prove that some Arabs were worshipping the Moon-God in Pre-Islamic Times.

But Shabir cannot rest with this reality. He must drag a red herring across the trail to divert attention from the crucial point. He argues over whether some minor artifacts are moon-god idols. The question of whether they were idols or not has no logical bearing on my point that an *Arabian temple to the Moon-God was dug up by Thompson*. The arguments over whether this or that broken statue is an idol does *not logically* affect this reality. Shabir does not refute or even deny Thompson's claim that she discovered a Moon-God temple in Arabia.

Shabir complains about my citations from such books as *The Ancient Near East: A New Anthology of Texts and Pictures*, *The Bible As History in Pictures*, and *Archaeology of The Bible*. I use them as illustrations of the vast scope of astral worship in the ancient world. Why does he whine about these citations?

Shabir shows his true ignorance by not understanding that Baal and other ancient deities were *astral* deities of the moon, sun and stars. He does not understand that the gender of the Moon-God and the Sun-God flipped from male to female at times. For the majority of time, the Moon-God was viewed as a male deity. But sometimes the Moon was viewed as female. The name of the Moon-God changed from culture to culture. The Moon-God could be described as a storm god in some cultures. Thus his argument falls to the ground because Baal was an astral deity connected to the worship of the moon and the sun, depending on by whom, when and where he was worshipped.

I have successfully documented that the Moon-God had many different names such as Nana, Hubal, Sin, etc. I also showed that he was also called Il or Ilah, which according to Coon and others, became Allah.

I must also point out that some scholars refer to Allah as a "name," while others use the word "title." The fact that pagan deities were given the title "daughters of Allah" and yet had personal names such as Al-Lat, Al-Uzza and Manat, is not a contradiction.

Why am I bringing this up? Shabir spends much time on the issue of whether I said that Allah was a "name" or a "title." Why did he waste time on such an irrelevant issue? It was another red herring! Whether or not I used "name" or "title" has no logical bearing on what I am saying about the history of Allah. Even Shabir must acknowledge that every title is a name!

Another fallacy practiced by Shabir is arguing in a circle. For example, there is a Pre-Islamic inscription where Sin had a father. Shabir rejects this as a reference to Allah because, according to Post-Islamic theology, Allah has no father. But he is begging the question at this point.

Shabir goes on to claim that since the Moon-God Sin is said to have a father, this refutes "my" idea that Allah was viewed as the "high" god by pagan Arabs. He then announces, "This again disproves Morey." Several comments are in order.

1. Why does he assume that Allah in Pre-Islamic times was not viewed as having a father by the pagans? On what grounds does he constantly read Post-Islamic ideas into Pre-Islamic inscriptions? If pagan Arabs thought that Allah had a wife and daughters, why wouldn't they think he had a father and a mother as well?

2. That Allah was viewed as a high god or even as the highest god by the Meccan pagans is not "my" idea. This is an observation made by many scholars long before I studied Islam. Shabir's fight is not with me but with the many scholars who hold to that position.

3. That the "high god" had a father does not logically imply that he was not viewed as the high god. Gods and goddesses come and go in ancient mythology.

Another problem in Shabir's booklet is that he argues that since Allah is not listed in some inscriptions along with other names for the Moon-God, this means Allah is not a name for the Moon-God. He concludes, "These inscriptions show that the Moon-god was not

Allah." But he is arguing from silence once again. It is logically irrelevant whether the Arabic word Allah appears or does not appear in some non-Arabic inscription. In the end, Shabir admits,

> "Morey was successful in proving that moon worship was prevalent in South Arabia before Islam."

Read his words several times. Did you see what he says? After calling me "deceptive" and "dishonest," in the end he admits that I was right!!!

He also commits the "Tit for Tat" fallacy of arguing that if Islam falls because Allah was originally the Moon-God, then Judaism goes down with it as some liberal scholars feel that Elohim started out as an astral deity. But the issue of whether Elohim started out as the Moon-God has no *logical* bearing on whether Allah began as the Moon-God. He is using Elohim as a red herring to divert attention from Allah.

At the end of his booklet, Shabir reveals his main error:

> "Even if he [Morey] was able to show that the North Arabs in Mecca worshipped the Moon-god, and even if he was able to show that they used to call this Moon-god Allah, this still does not prove that Allâh in Islam is a Moon-god. To prove or disprove this he needs to show what the Qur'ân teaches about moon worship.

> "The Qur'ân, however, clearly refutes moon-worship. The Qur'ân says: Adore not the sun and the moon, but adore Allâh who created them..." (Qur'ân 41:37). This statement reveals that Shabir's entire booklet is based on a

straw man of his own imagination. I have never said that Muslims today consciously worship the Moon. I have refuted this straw man in my booklet, *The Logical Fallacies Made by Muslims Apologists*. Since Shabir is fighting a figment of his imagination, his booklet is thus an exercise in futility.

CONCLUSION

While I am honored that Shabir has spent so much time attacking me personally, his character assassination is a failure due to his many logical fallacies. We pray that Shabir will turn from his false god, false prophet and false revelation to the one true God, true Prophet and true revelation. To the Holy Trinity be all the Glory! Amen!

GENERAL BIBLIOGRAPHY

'Abdallah 'Abd al-Fadi, *Is the Qur'an Infallible?* (Light of Life, Austria).

William F. Campbell M.D., *The Qur'an and the Bible in the Light of History and Science* (Middle East Resources, Upper Darby, PA, 1986).

Claude A. Clegg III, *An Original Man: The Life and Times of Elijah Muhammad* (St. Martin's Press, New York, NY, 1997).

'Ali Dashti, *Twenty Three Years: A Study of the Prophetic Career of Mohammad* (George Allen & Unwin Ltd, London, UK, 1985).

Paul Fregosi, *Jihad in the West: Muslim Conquests from the 7th to the 21st Centuries* (Prometheus Books, Amherst, NY, 1998).

Jan Goodwin, *Price of Honor: Muslim Women Lift the Veil of Silence on the Islamic World* (Little, Brown & Company, Canada, 1994).

Alfred Guillaume, *Islam* (Penguin Group, London, England, 1956).

Arthur J. Magida, *Prophet of Rage: A Life of Louis Farrakhan and His Nation* (BasicBooks, New York, NY, 1996).

Betty Mahmoody with William Hoffer, *Not Without My Daughter* (St. Martin's Press, New York, NY, 1987).

Judith Miller, *God Has Ninety-Nine Names: Reporting from a Militant Middle East* (Simon & Schuster, New York, NY, 1996).

William M. Miller, *A Christian's Response to Islam,* Presbyterian and Reformed Publishing Co., Phillipsburg, NJ, 1980).

Robert Morey, *The Islamic Invasion: Confronting the World's Fastest Growing Religion* (Christian Scholars Press, Las Vegas, NV, 1992).

G. J. O. Moshay, *Who is the Allah?* (Dorchester House Publications, Bucks, UK, 1995).

The Early Christian-Muslim Dialogue: A Collection of Documents from the First Three Islamic Centuries (632 – 900 A.D.): Translations with Commentary, ed. N. A. Newman (Interdisciplinary Biblical Research Institute, Hatfield, PA, 1993).

Rudolph Peters, *The Jihad in Classical and Modern Times* (Markus Wiener Publishers, Princeton, NJ, 1996).

Rev. W. St. Clair-Tisdall, M.A., *The Sources of Islam* (The message for Muslims Trust).

Jean Sasson, *Princess: A True Story of Life Behind the Veil in Saudi Arabia* (William Morrow and Company, Inc., New York, NY, 1992).

The Origins of the Koran: Classic Essays on Islam's Holy Book, ed. Ibn Warraq (Prometheus Books, Amherst, NY, 1998).

The Quest for the Historical Muhammad, ed. and trans. Ibn Warraq (Prometheus Books, Amherst, NY, 2000).

Ibn Warraq, *Why I Am Not a Muslim* (Prometheus Books, Amherst, NY, 1995).

W. Montgomery Watt, *Muhammad's Mecca: History in the Qur'an* (Edinburgh University Press, Edinburgh, 1988).

Samuel M. Zwemer, *The Moslem Doctrine of God: An Essay on the Character and Attributes of Allah According to the Koran and Orthodox Tradition* (American Tract Society, 1905).

The Islamic Invasion

This book is the first fully documented refutation of Islam in over a century. Over one hundred errors in the Qur'an are revealed. Dr. Morey proves that Allah is a false god, Muhammad a false prophet and the Qur'an is not the Word of God. This book deals with the "Black Muslims" as well as orthodox Islam. It has been translated into Swedish Norwegian, Danish, Farsi and Spanish with four more languages in preparation.

"Here is a book that concisely tells what Islam is ... and what it isn't! I found it absorbing, clear and very helpful. It is a readable expose of a major world religion that is a threat to our basic freedoms. I wish every Evangelical who is concerned about Muslim evangelism would read this book and pass it along to a friend."—**Dr. Erwin, Moody Church**

"Morey is a careful scholar whose statements we have learned to trust. If you want a reliable, trustworthy study of Islam, this is the book for you. Morey consulted every book in the Library of Congress; he read widely and digested carefully. This volume is the fruit of his labors. Even if you didn't want the book to assist you in reaching Muslims (which we hope you will), you still need to read it carefully in order to understand what is going on in the Middle East in our day. **—The Biblical Evangelist**

"Superb! Absolutely outstanding! This book is coherent, easy to read, comprehensive, touching every major concept of Islam while retaining brevity. It is succinct, giving just basic information without getting bogged down with minutiae; yet having ample references for anyone who wants to check its accuracy." **—Dr. Herbert Ehrenstein**
Eternity Magazine

To order, send check or money order in the amount of $14.95 plus $6.00 (S&H):
Faith Defenders
P. O. Box 7447, Orange CA 92863
Or call: 1(800) 41-TRUTH
Or go on line at: www.faithdefenders.com

When Is It Right to Fight?

Is it ever right to fight?
Does the Bible prohibit self-defense?
What does it mean to
"turn the other cheek?"

Paul wrote, "If it is possible, as far as it depends on you, live at peace with everyone" (Rom. 12:18). What if it isn't possible? What if others will not live at peace with us? Is there a time when force is necessary to resist evil? Is there such a thing as a "just war"? Can war be reconciled with the sacredness of human life?

In light of the War on Terrorism, these questions are relevant to all who care about the issues of peace, justice and freedom. Dr. Morey answers such questions in this incisive critique of pacifism in the light of the Bible and of church history.

"Dr. Morey's book is one of the best books on the subject of a 'just war' that I have read."   **—Dr. John W. Whitehead**
                                                                 Rutherford Institute

[This book] "annihilates the position of pacifism. The quotations alone (representing tremendous research) are worth several times the price of the book."   **—The Biblical Evangelist**

To order, send check or money order in the amount of $10.95 plus $6.00 (S&H):

Faith Defenders

P. O. Box 7447, Orange CA 92863
Or call: 1(800) 41-TRUTH
Or go on line at: www.faithdefenders.com

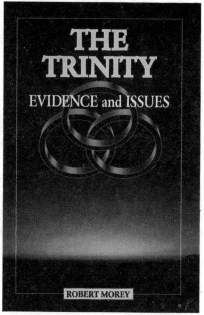

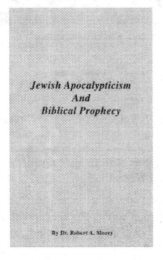